*For the Love of Language:
Recitation the Waldorf Way*

Other books by Roberto Trostli

Rhythms of Learning
Physics the Waldorf Way
Chemistry the Waldorf Way
Home Surroundings the Waldorf Way
Thy Will Be Done—the Task of the College of Teachers in Waldorf Schools
and
Teaching Language Arts in the Waldorf School

For the Love of Language

Recitation the Waldorf Way

A Manual for Teachers
Grades 5–8

Roberto Trostli

Printed with support from the Waldorf Curriculum Fund

Published by:

Waldorf Publications at the
Research Institute for Waldorf Education
351 Fairview Avenue, Suite 625
Hudson, NY 12534

Title: *For the Love of Language: Recitation the Waldorf Way*
     A Manual for Teachers: Grades 5–8
Author: Roberto Trostli
Layout: Ann Erwin
Proofreader: Ruth Riegel

ISBN #978-1-963686-05-0

Copyright © 2024 by Roberto Trostli and Waldorf Publications

All rights reserved. No part of this book may be reproduced in any form or medium without written permission of the author. Only brief passages may be quoted for purposes of reviewing the book without written permission from the author.

Table of Contents

Introduction 7

Recitation in Fifth Grade 9
    Yearly Verses 10
    Recitations from History 12
    Serious Poems 19
    Humorous Poems 27
    Speech Exercises 33
    Tongue Twisters 38

Recitation in Sixth Grade 42
    Yearly Verses 43
    Recitations from History 45
    Serious Poems 52
    Humorous Poems 59
    Speech Exercises 65
    Tongue Twisters 69

Recitation in Seventh Grade 76
    Yearly Verses 78
    Recitations from the Curriculum 79
    Lyrical Poems 85
    Narrative Poems 93
    Speech Exercises 100
    Tongue Twisters 105

Recitation in Eighth Grade 110
    Yearly Verses 112
    Poetry and Prose Selections 113
    Speech Exercises 147
    Tongue Twisters 152

References 155

Introduction

"In the beginning was the Word." – Saint John

Speech allows us to experience and express our humanity. It allows us to get to know ourselves and others, preserve memories, and develop our thoughts and concepts. Speech allows us to communicate with others and to experience the words of those who came before us.

Our speech as teachers has a profound effect on our students. The clarity of our speech helps them develop their thinking. The expressiveness of our speech helps them develop their feelings. And the directness of our speech helps them develop their wills. We should not underestimate how much our students learn from the way we teachers speak and express ourselves.

Our students spend many hours listening to us; therefore, the more mindful we can be of our speech, the better we can help them on their path of becoming themselves. Our students also spend many hours speaking to us and to others, so when we help them speak clearly, expressively, and powerfully, we help them become more effective communicators.

Much of your work with your students with recitation will be done during the Morning Exercises. The verses, poems, and prose passages that students will learn will give them a rich literary heritage that will expand their horizons. By learning these works by heart, your students will enrich their souls and will store away treasures that they will appreciate for many years to come. Work with speech will also help your students develop their enunciation and expressiveness, and it will build their confidence to speak in front of others. Finally, because speech is a social art, your work with speech will nourish the class community and strengthen the students' relationships with one another and with you.

This book was written to help you work more joyfully and effectively on recitation with your students. Because the chapters are divided by grade level and the selections are grouped by themes, it should assist you in your preparation. Each chapter includes suggestions for how to work with introductions, and many of the selections include background material that will provide some context for the selections. Finally, I include my innovative approaches to speech exercises and tongue twisters to challenge and delight your students.

The selections in this book were derived from my many decades of class teaching. They reflect my interests and my sense of humor and are not meant to be prescriptive. I encourage you to go beyond these selections to find the poetry and prose works that speak to your students. I also hope that you will develop your own ways of working with speech exercises and tongue twisters, because whatever you develop yourself will stimulate your enthusiasm for teaching and will engage your students most fully.

Note: Because this book was written for teachers, not the general public, permission for inclusion was not sought from the authors or publishers. I tried to keep the selections accurate and true to the originals, but there may be errors. Corrections should be forwarded to Waldorf Publications, Patrice Maynard, oneill@waldorf-research.org.

– Roberto Trostli
Richmond, VA, 2024

Recitation in Fifth Grade

Fifth grade tends to be the most harmonious year of elementary school because the students are at a balance point—leaving childhood behind but not yet experiencing the turbulence of adolescence. Fifth graders are very receptive to what they study. They are enthusiastic about learning and eager for academic, artistic, and athletic challenges. Most fifth graders are sociable and accepting, well able to work harmoniously as a group. This allows us to accomplish a great deal in recitation because we can call on students to be present as individuals and, at the same time, to work with their classmates as a group.

The recitation curriculum for fifth grade includes selections from history, nature study, and geography; serious and humorous poems; speech exercises and tongue twisters. The selections from history include excerpts from Ancient India, Ancient Persia, Ancient Egypt, and Ancient Greece. Some of the excerpts are in the original language, which will give students a vivid experience of the cultures they are studying. The selections from nature study and geography reinforce and extend what the students are learning; the serious and humorous poems present them with contrasting ways to express ourselves; and the speech exercises and tongue twisters challenge students to develop mobility in their thinking and in their speech.

Before beginning to work on a recitation, you should introduce it. Recitations about curricular subjects do not need an introduction because the Main Lesson presentation will have provided the context. For all other selections, introductions should include the title and the author of the work, and, if you wish, something about the author's life. Then you should provide a brief summary of the work and speak about the important images, people, or events. If the work is in a language other than English, your introduction should provide enough of a foundation for students to appreciate the correspondence between the original and the translation.

Poems with particularly meaningful themes or characters warrant a more thorough introduction. For these introductions, you should comment freely about the work, expressing your ideas and opinions. If it seems appropriate, you can also involve the students in a discussion about the theme or characters, which will help them connect with the verse and appreciate it more fully. Such discussions strengthen the class community because students get to know each other better, and they deepen our bond with our students because they hear us expressing what we think and believe.

In Discussion 6 of *Discussions with Teachers*, Rudolf Steiner explained why we speak about a work *before* rather than *after* the students have heard it, and he demonstrated how to introduce a fable or a poem. If you are new to this approach, I encourage you to try it. Although you may feel a bit awkward at first, you will discover how well it works.

Fifth graders can easily recite in unison, so they are ready for greater challenges. We should therefore work with speech exercises in groups and include variations that require students to hold their own.

In addition to speech exercises, tongue twisters can be used to challenge the students' memories, refine their enunciation, and can be used as a warm-up for longer recitations. Because fifth graders are able to master tongue twisters so quickly, they should be performed with variations and alternated frequently. Detailed instructions about various ways to work with tongue twisters may be found on pages 38–41, 69–75, 105–109, and 152–154.

I recommend that the Morning Exercises continue to be coordinated with the Main Lesson blocks when possible, because this enhances the students' experience of the block, and the monthly rhythm allows the material to be taken up fully, but they may not fit neatly into the block schedule. Although Morning Exercises are important, they should not exceed about 30 minutes per day. When we spend too much time on them, students can become less attentive and responsive and may have difficulty concentrating on their work. Your class will benefit from the Morning Exercise routines, but we need to remember that they are only a preparation for—not a major component of—the Main Lesson.[1]

YEARLY VERSES

Verses that are used throughout the year have a special place in the speech curriculum, and our daily repetition of these verses affirms their importance and worth.

A typical fifth-grade Main Lesson begins with announcements, class housekeeping, and perhaps a brief check-in (although this might wait until later in the year or until sixth grade.) All of these should precede the recitation of the Morning Verse so that it can serve as a formal beginning to the Main Lesson. I encourage the upper grades in your school to use the same version of the Morning Verse in order to strengthen the sense of community among the students. I have therefore not included any versions of the Morning Verse because it is important for each school to choose the translation they prefer.

Some of the yearly verses can be recited for several years. All of my classes recited "There Lives in Me an Image," at the end of the Morning Exercises and "May Wisdom Shine through Me," at the end of Main Lesson, for our entire eight-year journey, and we ended the day with "At the Ringing of the Bells" in grades five through eight. By reciting these verses over so many years, I hoped that their ideals would be planted in the students' hearts and bear fruit in the course of their lives.

---

[1] Suggestions for creating Morning Exercises may be found at the end of this chapter.

Angelus Silesius (1624–1677) was the name that Johann Scheffler adopted when he became a Catholic priest. He composed many religious poems that expressed his mystical beliefs.

There Lives in Me an Image
Angelus Silesius

There lives in me an image,
Of all that I should be;
Until I have become it,
My heart is never free.

May Wisdom Shine through Me
Rudolf Steiner

May wisdom shine through me,
May love glow within me,
May strength permeate me,
That in me may arise
A helper of humankind,
A server of holy things,
Selfless and true.

At the Ringing of the Bells
Rudolf Steiner

To wonder at beauty,
Stand guard over truth,
Look up to the noble,
Decide for the good—
Leads us on our journey
To goals for our life:
To right in our doing;
To peace in our feeling;
To light in our thought.
And teaches us trust
In the guidance of God;
In all that there is—
In the world-wide All,
In the soul's deep soil.

RECITATIONS FROM HISTORY

The study of Ancient India, Ancient Persia, Babylonia, Chaldea, Egypt, and Greece provide the context for recitations from these cultures. The introductions can therefore focus on specific aspects of the recitation.

The "Hymn of Creation" from the Rig Veda is a compelling recitation because it portrays the creation myth so clearly. I encourage you to speak or chant it in the original language, because the sounds and the mood convey a great deal, even if all of the words are not understood. Examples of this verse's proper pronunciation can be found online.

> **Hymn of Creation**
> *from the Rig Veda*
>
> Nāsad āsīn no sad āsīt tadānīṁ
> Nāsīd rajo no vyomā paro yat |
> Kim āvarīvaḥ kuha kasya śarmann
> Ambhaḥ kim āsīd gahanaṁ gabhīram
>
> Then even nothingness was not, nor existence,
> There was no air then, nor the heavens beyond it.
> What covered it? Where was it?
> In whose keeping
> Was there then cosmic water, in depths unfathomed?
>
> Then there was neither death nor immortality
> Nor was there then the torch of night and day.
> The One breathed windlessly and self-sustaining.
> There was that One then, and there was no other.

This Persian verse clearly expresses the nature of the human being, living between light and darkness, and our affirms that our task is to transform the earth and its creatures through love.

> **From Ancient Persia**
>
> Bear the sun to the earth!
> You, O human being
> Are set between light and darkness.
> Be a warrior of the light!
> Into a radiant diamond
> Transform the plants,
> Transform the animals,
> Transform yourself.

Ahura Mazda and Ahriman are the embodiments of light and darkness in Persian mythology. In your introduction, you might review the qualities and the various names given to these two deities. The *Gathas of Zarathustra* include holy hymns that glorify Ahura Mazda and others that express the qualities that must be cultivated to lead a virtuous life.

Gathas of Zarathustra (excerpt)

In the flaming fire we worship thee,
    Master of Wisdom,
    Lord of Light,
    Ahura-Mazda,
O Spirit speak to us
    In the glory of the Sun, O Lord of Life.

From the regions of the North
From the regions of the South,
Forth rushed Ahriman the deadly,
And the demons of darkness, the evil-doers;
    Thus spake Ahriman, the deadly Deceiver:
    "Kill him, destroy him, Hated Zarathustra."

Thus spake Zarathustra:
    "The word of Ahura-Mazda is my weapon
With his sword will I strike
The Holy word of the Lord of Light,
The living word of Creation."
Forth fled Ahriman, the Deceiver
    And the wicked evil-doing Demons
    Into the depths of outer darkness.

This excerpt from the *Zend Avesta* expresses the Persian view of the relationship of human beings to the earth.

Zend Avesta (excerpt)

O Maker of the material world, thou Holy one!
Which are the places where the Earth feels most happy?

It is the place whereon one of the faithful erects a house with a priest within,
With cattle, with a wife, with children, and good herds within.

It is the place where one of the faithful sows most corn, grass, and fruit,
Where he waters ground that is dry, or drains ground that is too wet.

It is the place where there is most increase of flocks and herds.
And the place where flocks and herds yield most dung.

This speech from "The Epic of Gilgamesh" captures the essence of Gilgamesh's quest to understand the power of death. If you recite this selection after the students have heard the epic, the introduction need not provide background information, though it might still be worthwhile to discuss the theme of mortality. You can find recitations about other themes in Bernarda Bryson's *Gilgamesh: Man's First Story*. Although this is a retelling rather than a translation, Bryson's language captures the narrative's epic nature.

The Epic of Gilgamesh (excerpt)
Bernarda Bryson

Listen to me, O Utnapishtim!
I had a friend dearer to me than a brother.
Day and night we went together;
Together we roamed over the wild steppes and through the forests,
Hunting and wrestling with wild animals.
Together we demolished the monster Humbaba that daily threatened our city;
Together we killed the Bull of Heaven that had been sent against us to destroy us.
Everywhere we walked together, sharing all dangers and all delights.

Then death came to Enkidu: the fate of mortal men overtook him!
He did not die in battle like some hero;
He didn't die of illness or venerable old age;
The earth came up and seized him!

Then, O Utnapishtim, I was overcome by terror and by grief.
Alone, I set out over the wild places of the earth to find you, my ancestor.
For I have been told that you were chosen to join the assembly of the gods,
And that you know the secret of life and death.

Tell me now, O Utnapishtim,
Must my brother remain for all the years lying at the center of the earth?
Will he never again see the face of the sun, and must I too die?

Robert Hillyer (1895–1961) was an American poet and a professor of English literature. "He Walketh by Day" from Hillyer's *The Coming Forth by Day: An Anthology of Poems from the Egyptian Book of the Dead* expresses the nature of the divine.

He Walketh by Day
Robert Hillyer, translator

I am yesterday, today, and tomorrow,
The divine hidden soul who created the gods
And who feedeth the blessed.

I am lord of the risers from death,
Whose forms are lamps in the house of the dead,
Whose shrine is the earth.

When the sky is illumined with crystal,
Then gladden my road and broaden my path
And clothe me in light.

Keep me safe from the sleeper in darkness,
When eventide closeth the eyes of the god
And the door by the wall.

In the dawn I have opened the sycamore;
My form is the form of all women and men;
My spirit is God.

The next two hymns capture the ancient Egyptians' reverence for Ra, the king of the gods and the father of all creation. The hymns are even more powerful when accompanied by expressive gestures.

Hymn to the Sun
from Ancient Egypt

Hail to thee, O Ra, O perfect and eternal one.
Great Hawk that fliest with the rising Sun.
Between the turquoise sycamores thou risest young forever,
Thine image flashing on the bright celestial river.
Thou passes through the portals that close behind the night,
Gladdening the souls of them that lie in sorrow,
The true of word, the quiet of heart arise to drink thy light,
Thou art today and yesterday, thou art tomorrow.

Hymn in Praise of Ra
from the Book of the Dead

Beautiful is Thy awakening
    Thou hawk of the morning
Thou glorious Being
    That openest Thine eyes
Thou lofty Being
    Whose course is not known to man
Thou image great
    The horizon's first born.
Exceedingly high Thou art
    And beyond man's reach
That risest from the ocean as a bird
    That drivest away darkness
And bringest light
    He overcometh the Serpent of Evil
In the name of Ra.

I encourage you to teach your students a few lines of Greek to have them experience the musical nature of the language. The correct pronunciation can be found online.

There are many translations for the opening lines of *The Iliad*. I am partial to the one by Professor Lombardo because it captures the pithiness of the original lines.

Opening Lines of **The Iliad**
Homer

μῆνιν ἄειδε θεὰ Πηληϊάδεω Ἀχιλῆος
οὐλομένην, ἣ μυρί' Ἀχαιοῖς ἄλγε' ἔθηκε,
πολλὰς δ' ἰφθίμους ψυχὰς Ἄϊδι προΐαψεν
ἡρώων, αὐτοὺς δὲ ἑλώρια τεῦχε κύνεσσιν
οἰωνοῖσί τε, Διὸς δ' ἐτελείετο βουλή,
ἐξ οὗ δὴ τὰ πρῶτα διαστήτην ἐρίσαντε
Ἀτρεΐδης τε ἄναξ ἀνδρῶν καὶ δῖος Ἀχιλλεύς.

Menin aeide Thea, Peleiadeo Akhileos
Oulomenen, he muri Akhaiois alge etheken
Pollas diphthimous pseukhas Aidi proiapsen
Heroon, autous de heloria teukhe kunessiv
Oionoisi te daita, Dio d'eteleieto boule
Ex hou de ta prota diasteten erisante
Atreides te anax andron kai dios Akhilleus.

Opening Lines of **The Iliad**
translated by Stanley Lombardo

Sing, Goddess, Achilles' rage,
Black and murderous, that cost the Greeks
Incalculable pain, pitched countless souls
Of heroes into Hades' dark,
And left their bodies to rot as feasts
For dogs and birds, as Zeus' will was done.
Begin with the clash between Agamemnon—
The Greek warlord—and godlike Achilles.

Opening Lines of **The Iliad**
translated by Charles Stuart Calverley (1831-1884)

Sing, O daughter of heaven, of Peleus's son, of Achilles
Him whose terrible wrath brought thousand woes on Achaia.
Many a stalwart soul did it hurl untimely to Hades,
Souls of the heroes of old: and their bones lay strown on the sea-sands,
Prey to the vulture and dog. Yet was Zeus fulfilling a purpose;
Since that far-off day, when in hot strife parted asunder
Atreus's sceptred son, and the chos'n of heaven, Achilles.

In many Waldorf schools, students participate in a Greek Pentathlon. During this event, students may recite odes to the gods of the city states such as this "Ode to Zeus." In some schools, students compose their own oaths or prayers that can be recited during the weeks prior to the Pentathlon.

Ode to Zeus

To you all honor O Olympia
Guided by the wisdom of Zeus,
Grant that my skills reap triumph.
For my limbs, I ask grace and beauty
For my heart, Courage and honesty
Know, my all-powerful Zeus,
That my efforts will never falter.

Olympic Oath

O radiant Apollo
Help me to participate
With grace and beauty.
Bless me with Strength
So that my javelin will fly
As wonderfully as an eagle.
Help me run like a graceful deer.
Let my discus fly through the air
With power that matches
Your mighty swan.
I hope your power fills me
As I strive to reach my goal.

Eileen Hutchins (1902–1987) was a founding teacher at the Elmfield School in Stourbridge, England. As a class and high school teacher, she developed the literature curriculum for English-speaking Waldorf schools. Eileen Hutchins wrote extensively on Waldorf education and edited *Child and Man* for many years. During your introduction to her poem about Hercules, you might draw the students' attention to the contrasting alternating lines.

Hercules
Eileen Hutchins

Who is this who cometh as in conquest?
    Strong he strides and free.
Light of glory gleams around his temples,
    More than man is he.
Dark has been the danger of his daring,
    Fierce the first and fell;

None can know the fashion of his faring
    Hither out of hell.
Who is this who cometh as in conquest?
    Strong he strides and free.
Light of glory gleams around his temples,
    Man and god is he.

Roy Wilkinson (1911–2007) was a highly regarded English author and lecturer on Waldorf education, and his books and curriculum guides provide detailed advice for teachers. In your introduction, you might ask the students what they remember from your presentation about Prometheus's contributions to humanity.

Hymn to Prometheus
Roy Wilkinson

Hail to Prometheus, the Titan,
    the helper of man and creator.
Clay was the substance he used
    and in likeness of gods then he shaped it.
Goodness and evil from hearts
    of the beasts in man's breast he enfolded.
Fire he brought down from the realms
    of the skies to perfect his creation.
Movement of stars he explained
    to the wondering earth-dwelling people.
Numbers he taught them to use
    and the plants which heal sickness he showed them.
Symbols he taught them to write,
    representing the sounds of their speaking.
Building of ships he did teach
    and the training of beasts to man's service.
Into the depths of the earth
    did he guide men to find precious metals.
Zeus he defied and brought fire
    down again when the god would deny men.
Torment and anguish he suffered
    for harsh was the fate decreed for him.
Bound to a cliff overhanging
    a sinister cleft was Prometheus.
Bravely the Titan endured
    and at length one arrived to release him.

Edith Hamilton was a celebrated classicist who wrote extensively about ancient mythology. In her translation from *Prometheus Bound*, she captures the power of Aeschylus's images and the eloquence of his speech.

Prometheus Bound (excerpt)
Aeschylus, Edith Hamilton, translator

An end to words. Deeds now.
The world is shaken.
The deep and secret way of thunder
Is rent apart.
Fiery wreaths of lighting flash;
Whirlwinds toss the swirling dust.
The blasts of all the winds are battling in the air,
And sky and sea are one.
On me the tempest falls,
It does not make me tremble.
O holy Mother Earth, O air and sun
Behold me.
I am wronged.

SERIOUS POEMS

Fiona Macleod was the pseudonym for William Sharp (1855–1905), a Scottish poet who managed to keep Fiona Macleod's identity secret for many years. In your introduction, you might speak with the students about the power of repetition in this recitation.

Lines from Invocation of Peace
Fiona Macleod

Deep peace, pure white of the moon to you;
Deep peace, pure green of the grass to you;
Deep peace, pure brown of the earth to you;
Deep peace, pure grey of the dew to you.
Deep peace, pure blue of the sky to you
Deep peace of the running wave to you.
Deep peace of the flowing air to you,
Deep peace of the quiet earth to you.

In second grade students may have heard about the life Saint Francis. In the introduction to "Desiderata," you might speak about what a remarkable man he was and the virtues he embodied. You can point out the pairs of words in this prayer that highlight these virtues. Note: Desiderata means "that which is wanted or needed."

Desiderata
Saint Francis

Lord, make me an instrument of Thy peace.
Where there is hatred, let me sow love,
Where there is injury, pardon,
Where there is doubt, faith,
Where there is despair, hope,
Where there is darkness, light
And where there is sadness, joy.

O Divine Master, grant that I
May not so much seek
To be consoled as to console,
To be understood as to understand,
To be loved as to love.
For it is in giving that we receive,
It is pardoning that we are pardoned,
It is in dying that we are born to eternal life.

Henry Wadsworth Longfellow (1808–1882) was one of the most beloved American poets of the 19th century. Some of his most famous poems include "Paul Revere's Ride," "The Song of Hiawatha," and "Evangeline." You may wish to have your students learn or read the prelude from "Evangeline" because it is written in hexameter, the poetic meter used by Homer and other ancient Greek authors.

Prelude from Evangeline: A Tale of Acadie
Henry Wadsworth Longfellow

This is the forest primeval. The murmuring pines and the hemlocks,
Bearded with moss, and in garments green, indistinct in the twilight,
Stand like Druids of eld, with voices sad and prophetic,
Stand like harpers hoar, with beards that rest on their bosoms.
Loud from its rocky caverns, the deep-voiced neighboring ocean
Speaks, and in accents disconsolate answers the wail of the forest.

Many of poems by Emily Dickinson (1830–1886) are suitable for grade-school students because they capture a moment or a mood in just a few lines. Emily Dickinson's poems are highly pictorial. In your introduction, you might ask the students to name some of autumn's attributes and connect them with Emily Dickinson's images. You might also draw their attention to her use of comparatives to draw a distinction between Autumn and the previous months.

Autumn
Emily Dickinson

The morns are meeker than they were,
    The nuts are getting brown;
The berry's cheek is plumper,
    The rose is out of town.

The maple wears a gayer scarf,
    The field a scarlet gown.
Lest I should be old-fashioned,
    I'll put a trinket on.

Hallowe'en continues to be one of the students' favorite holidays, and if your class didn't learn the Hallowe'en poems in previous chapters, some of them might be learned in fifth grade. When you introduce "The Witch's House," you might show the students how Laura Benét (1884–1979) uses words to paint a haunting, dramatic picture.

The Witch's House
Laura Benét

Its wicked little windows leer
    Beneath a moldy thatch,
And village children come and peer
    Before they lift the latch.

A one-eyed crow hops to the door,
    Fat spiders crowd the pane,
And dark herbs scattered on the floor
    Waft fragrance down the lane.

It sits so low, the little hutch,
    So secret, shy and squat,
As if in its mysterious clutch
    It nursed one knew not what.

That beggars passing by the ditch
    Are haunted by desire
To force the door, and see the witch
    Vanish in flames of fire.

"The Sea Wolf" by Violet McDougal (1893–1981) appeals to fifth graders because of its strong images and dramatic undertone. When introducing this poem, I suggest giving a picture of the ocean with the fishermen on the surface and the Sea Wolf lurking below. Draw the students' attention to the effect of the powerful verbs in the third and fourth stanzas and the way that tension is released at the end of the poem. This poem is very effective in performance.

The Sea Wolf
Violet McDougal

The fishermen say, when your catch is done
And you're sculling in with the tide,
You must take great care that the Sea Wolf's share
Is tossed to him overside.

They say that the Sea Wolf rides, by day,
Unseen on the crested waves,
And the sea mists rise from his cold green eyes
When he comes from his salt sea caves.

The fishermen say, when it storms at night
And the great seas bellow and roar,
That the Sea Wolf rides on the plunging tides,
And you hear his howl at the door.

And you must throw open your door at once
And fling your catch to the waves,
Till he drags his share to his cold sea lair,
Straight down to his salt sea caves.

Then the storm will pass, and the still stars shine,
In peace—so the fishermen say—
But the Sea Wolf waits by the cold Sea Gates
For the dawn of another day.

Alfred Joyce Kilmer (1886–1918) was an American poet, journalist, and lecturer, who died in France in World War I. "Trees" is Kilmer's best-known poem, reportedly written one afternoon while looking down on a wooded hill. Although the poem has been criticized for its sentimentality, it conveys its message simply and effectively. Your introduction might mention that when human beings create, they are experiencing and expressing the divinity that dwells within us.

Trees
Joyce Kilmer

I think that I shall never see
A poem lovely as a tree.
A tree whose hungry mouth is prest
Against the earth's sweet flowing breast;
A tree that looks at God all day,
And lifts her leafy arms to pray;
A tree that may in summer wear
A nest of robins in her hair;
Upon whose bosom snow has lain;
Who intimately lives with rain.
Poems are made by fools like me,
But only God can make a tree.

Ben Jonson (1572–1637) was a very popular playwright, second only to his contemporary, William Shakespeare. Jonson also wrote lyric poetry, and "The Noble Nature" is the first stanza of an ode to the relationship between two Jonson's friends, one of whom who died young. The introduction to this poem might contrast the images of the ancient oak and the ephemeral lily, and students could discuss the value of a long life compared to a short life.

The Noble Nature
Ben Jonson

It is not growing like a tree
In bulk, doth make man better be;
Or standing long an oak, three hundred year
To fall a log at last, dry, bald, and sear:
   A lily of a day
   Is fairer far in May,
   Although it fall and die that night,—
   It was the plant and flower of Light.
In small proportions we just beauties see,
And in short measures life may perfect be.

In their study of the plant world, students will have learned how plants provide us with countless useful materials. In your introduction to this poem, you might review the practical uses of lumber in ships and houses and contrast these with the more inspirational uses of wood in a church spire or in the pole for the country's flag. This poem lends itself to dividing the lines among the students individually or in groups, but I suggest having the whole class pose the question "What do we plant when we plant the tree?" and the last line of each stanza, which answers that question.

What Do We Plant
Henry Abbey (1842-1911)

What do we plant when we plant the tree?
We plant the ship, which will cross the sea.
We plant the mast to carry the sails;
We plant the planks to withstand the gales -
The keel, the keelson, the beam, the knee;
We plant the ship when we plant the tree.

What do we plant when we plant the tree?
We plant the houses for you and me.
We plant the rafters, the shingles, the floors,
We plant the studding, the lath, the doors,
The beams and siding, all parts that be;
We plant the house when we plant the tree.

What do we plant when we plant the tree?
A thousand things that we daily see;
We plant the spire that out-towers the crag,
We plant the staff for our country's flag,
We plant the shade, from the hot sun free;
We plant all these when we plant the tree.

Christina Rossetti (1830–1894) was one of the foremost female poets of her day. One of her poems was set to music by Gustav Holst and became the much beloved Christmas carol—"In the Bleak Midwinter." In your introduction to "I Dug and Dug Amongst the Snow," you might contrast the apparent barrenness of a snowy waste with the lifeless desert.

I Dug and Dug Amongst the Snow
Christina Rossetti

I dug and dug amongst the snow,
And thought the flowers would never grow;
I dug and dug amongst the sand,
And still no green thing came to hand.
Melt, O snow! the warm winds blow
To thaw the flowers and melt the snow;
But all the winds from every land
Will rear no blossom from the sand.

Alfred, Lord Tennyson (1809–1892) was the most famous English poet of the Victorian era. In your introduction, you might tell the students that how Tennyson strove to capture the song of the throstle—or song thrush—by using rhythm and repetition. When working with this poem, try to get the tempo and the rhythm to emulate a bird song.

The Throstle
Alfred, Lord Tennyson

"Summer is coming, summer is coming,
I know it, I know it, I know it.
Light again, leaf again, life again, love again."
Yes, my wild little Poet.

Sing the new year in under the blue.
Last year you sang it as gladly.
"New, new, new, new!" Is it then so new
That you should carol so madly?

"Love again, song again, nest again, young again,"
Never a prophet so crazy!
And hardly a daisy as yet, little friend,
See there is hardly a daisy.

"Here again, here, here, here, happy year!"
Oh, warble unchidden, unbidden!
Summer is coming, is coming, my dear,
And all the winters are hidden.

Eugene Schwartz (1945–) was a class teacher at the Green Meadow Waldorf School for many years. In the introduction to this poem you might allude to the fact that natural phenomena reveal some of great mysteries of life. You might also discuss what we can learn from ants, bees, and butterflies.

Ant, Bee and Butterfly
Eugene Schwartz

Have you ever watched the humble ants
Cast up hillocks of dirt?
And carve out catacomb-like halls
Sequestered in the earth?
Within they form a little world,
So perfect in itself,
Where each the other serves and so
Ensouls the common wealth.
Rotting wood they turn to good,
Dead carrion make living,
While on her eggs their calm Queen broods;

Prime Mother, ever giving.
The busy bee asks not the aim
Nor purpose of his labor,
For in it he such sweetness finds
That the task itself he savors.
The bloom and bee, the bee and hive
Form a sweet trinity;
For through the bee the seed shall thrive,
And through the blossom lives the bee.
When the chrysalis seems most asleep
Or deathlike, she is weaving
On the warp and woof of her living loom
And her primal form receiving.
Then, as a golden butterfly,
Casting off the gray and cold,
She awakens, self-created,
Reborn, renewed and whole.

Marianne Moore (1887–1972) was one of the 20th century's foremost poets and literary critics. Like many of her poems, "A Jelly-Fish" is characterized by precise descriptions. In your introduction to this poem, you might speak with the students about the mysterious nature of the jellyfish, which can only be appreciated when observing it in the water.

A Jelly-Fish
Marianne Moore

Visible, invisible,
A fluctuating charm,
An amber-colored amethyst
Inhabits it; your arm
Approaches, and
It opens and
It closes;
You have meant
To catch it,
And it shrivels;
You abandon
Your intent—
It opens, and it
Closes and you
Reach for it—
The blue
Surrounding it
Grows cloudy, and
It floats away
From you.

HUMOROUS POEMS

Fifth graders enjoy plays on words, and they will be delighted by the linguistic anomalies presented in the next two poems. In your introduction to the first one, you might take up the theme of common plurals and create a list of some of the ones included in this poem. In your introduction to the second one, you might take up the inconsistencies in spelling and pronunciation among similar words. Both of these poems work well as assembly presentations because each couplet will amuse the audience.

Why English Is So Hard to Learn
James Donovan

We'll begin with box, and the plural is boxes;
But the plural of ox should be oxen, not oxes.
Then one fowl is goose, but two are called geese,
Yet the plural of moose should never be meese.

You may find a lone mouse or a nest full of mice,
Yet the plural of house is houses, not hice.
If the plural of man is always called men,
Why shouldn't the plural of pan be called pen?

The cow in the plural may be cows or kine,
But the plural of vow is vows, not vine.
I speak of my foot and show you my feet,
If I give you a boot, would a pair be called beet?

If one is a tooth, and a whole set are teeth,
Why shouldn't the plural of booth be called beeth?
If the singular is this and the plural is these,
Why shouldn't the plural of kiss be named kese?

Then one may be that, and three may be those,
Yet the plural of hat would never be hose;
We speak of a brother, and also of brethren,
But though we say mother, we never say methren.

The masculine pronouns are he, his and him,
But imagine the feminine she, shis, and shim!
So our English, I think, you all will agree,
Is the craziest language you ever did see.

English
T.S. Watt

I take it you already know
Of *tough* and *bough* and *cough* and *dough*?
Others may stumble, but not you
On *hiccough, thorough, slough,* and *through*?
Well done! And now you wish, perhaps
To learn of less familiar traps?

Beware of *heard*, a dreadful word
That looks like *beard* and sounds like *bird*.
And *dead*; it's said like *bed*, not *bead*;
For goodness sake, don't call it *deed*!
Watch out for *meat* and *great* and *threat*,
(They rhyme with *suite* and *straight* and *debt*)
A *moth* is not a moth in *mother*.
Nor *both* in *bother, broth* in *brother*.
And *here* is not a match for *there*.
And *dear* and *fear* for *bear* and *pear*.
And then there's *dose* and *rose* and *lose*—
Just look them up—and *goose* and *choose*.
And *cork* and *work* and *card* and *ward*,
And *font* and *front* and *word* and *sword*.
And *do* and *go*, then *thwart* and *cart*.
Come, come, I've hardly made a start.

A dreadful language? Why, man alive,
I'd learned to talk it when I was five,
And yet to write it, the more I tried,
I hadn't learned it at sixty-five!

Victor Borge (1909–2000) was a Danish-American entertainer who blended comedy with music. Many of his routines feature his virtuoso piano skills used in innovative ways. One of Victor Borge's most popular comedic routines is called "Audible Punctuation," where he assigns a sound to each of the punctuation marks. When he reads a passage, making the punctuation audible, the sounds and words create a wonderful comic blend. I have worked with a variation of audible punctuation with several classes, and the students loved it. Victor Borge's performances of "Audible Punctuation" can be found online.

Lewis Carroll was the pen name of Charles Lutwidge Dodgson (1832–1898), who was a mathematics professor at Oxford University. Lewis Carroll is best known for *Alice's Adventures in Wonderland* and its sequel, *Through the Looking Glass*. Dodgson enjoyed creating mathematical puzzles and riddles, and both of the Alice books include many such riddles in story form.

"Jabberwocky," which appeared in *Through the Looking Glass*, is probably the most famous nonsense poem in English. In this poem, Lewis Carroll coined many new words made up from parts of other words, e.g., "slithy" which is a combination of "lithe" and "slimy" or "frumious" which combines "fuming" and "furious." Fifth graders will enjoy learning "Jabberwocky" and deciphering its meaning.

There are several options for introducing this poem. You might read it to the students without much introduction and let them be surprised and amused. You might introduce it by saying that it contains a number of imaginary characters and original words, which will become clearer as the poem is read. Or you might do a thorough introduction to the author and the characters and explain some of the words. With this kind of introduction, the poem will make more sense but the element of surprise will be diminished.

This poem works very well as an assembly recitation, especially if it is dramatized.

Jabberwocky
Lewis Carroll

'Twas brillig, and the slithy toves
    Did gyre and gimble in the wabe;
All mimsy were the borogoves,
    And the mome raths outgrabe.

"Beware the Jabberwock, my son!
    The jaws that bite, the claws that catch!
Beware the Jubjub bird, and shun
    The frumious Bandersnatch!"

He took his vorpal sword in hand:
    Long time the manxome foe he sought.
So rested he by the Tumtum tree,
    And stood awhile in thought.

And as in uffish thought he stood,
    The Jabberwock, with eyes of flame,
Came whiffling through the tulgey wood,
    And burbled as it came!

One, two! One, two and through and through
    The vorpal blade went snicker-snack!
He left it dead, and with its head
    He went galumphing back.

"And hast thou slain the Jabberwock?
    Come to my arms, my beamish boy!
O frabjous day! Callooh! Callay!"
    He chortled in his joy.

'Twas brillig, and the slithy toves
    Did gyre and gimble in the wabe;
All mimsy were the borogoves,
    And the mome raths outgrabe.

The next two poems do not need introductions because they are readily understood and enjoyed at their first hearing.

A Tragic Story
William Makepeace Thackeray (1811–1863)

There lived a sage in days of yore
And he a handsome pigtail wore;
But wondered much and sorrowed more
    Because it hung behind him.

He mused upon this curious case,
And swore he'd change the pigtail's place,
And have it hanging at his face,
    Not dangling there behind him.

Says he, "The mystery I've found—
I'll turn me round,"—he turned him round;
    But still it hung behind him.

Then round, and round, and out and in,
All day the puzzled sage did spin;
In vain—it mattered not a pin,—
    The pigtail hung behind him.

And right, and left, and round about,
And up, and down, and in, and out,
He turned; but still the pigtail stout
    Hung steadily behind him.

And though his efforts never slack,
And though he twist, and twirl, and tack,
Alas! still faithful to his back
    The pigtail hangs behind him.

After the Party
William Wise (1923-)

Jonathan Blake
Ate too much cake,
He isn't himself today;
He's tucked up in bed
With a feverish head,
And he doesn't much care to play.

Jonathan Blake
Ate too much cake,
And three kinds of ice cream too—
From latest reports
He's quite out of sorts,
And I'm sure the reports are true.

I'm sorry to state
That he also ate
Six pickles, a pie and a pear;
In fact I confess
It's a reasonable guess
He ate practically everything there.

Yes, Jonathan Blake
Ate too much cake,
So he's not at his best today;
But there's no need for sorrow—
If you come back tomorrow,
I'm sure he'll be out to play.

Shel Silverstein (1930–1999) was a very well-known American songwriter, poet, and novelist, who wrote many volumes of children's poetry. His book, *The Giving Tree*, is one of the most popular works of 20th-century children's literature. In your introduction to this poem, you might review all of the common—and uncommon—ailments that could keep Peggy Ann at home on a day when she doesn't want to go to school.

Sick
Shel Silverstein

"I cannot go to school today,"
Said little Peggy Ann McKay.
"I have the measles and the mumps,
A gash, a rash, and purple bumps.

My mouth is wet, my throat is dry,
I'm going blind in my right eye.
My tonsils are as big as rocks,
I've counted sixteen chicken pox,
And there's one more—that's seventeen,
And don't you think my face looks green?
My leg is cut, my eyes are blue—
It might be instamatic flu.
I cough and sneeze and gasp and choke,
I'm sure that my left leg is broke—
My hip hurts when I move my chin,
My belly button's caving in,
My back is wrenched, my ankle's sprained,
My 'pendix pains each time it rains.
My nose is cold, my toes are numb,
I have a sliver in my thumb.
My neck is stiff, my voice is weak,
I hardly whisper when I speak.
My tongue is filling up my mouth,
I think my hair is falling out.
My elbow's bent, my spine ain't straight,
My temperature is one-o-eight.
My brain is shrunk, I cannot hear,
There is a hole inside my ear.
I have a hangnail, and my heart is—what?
What's that? What's that you say?
You say today is—Saturday?
G'bye, I'm going out to play!"

Fifth graders enjoy word play of all sorts. "Stately Verse" will tickle their interest and may inspire them to create other examples of words with humorous origins. A poem such as this requires little or no introduction except, maybe, to challenge the students to guess what state will be named at the end of the stanzas.

Stately Verse

If Mary goes far out to sea,
By wayward breezes fanned,
I'd like to know—can you tell me?—
Just where would Maryland?

If Tenny went high up in air
And looked o'er land and lea,
Looked here and there and everywhere,
Pray what would Tennessee?

I looked out of the window and
Saw Orry on the lawn;
He's not there now, and who can tell
Just where has Oregon?

Two girls were quarrelling one day
With garden tools, and so
I said, "My dears, let Mary rake
And just let Idaho."

An English lady had a steed.
She called him 'ighland Bay.
She rode for exercise, and thus
Rhode Island every day.

SPEECH EXERCISES

By fifth grade, students can easily recite poems with accompaniments and as rounds. These variations were introduced in fourth grade, but now they can be taken to new levels of difficulty and complexity. A further variation that requires focus and concentration is to work with quodlibets, as described on pages 34–36, 65–68, 100–103, and 152. Although suggestions are provided for some possible variations, I encourage you to create your own, and occasionally to challenge students to share ideas for making the speech exercise more interesting and fun.

"Whether the Weather" can be done as a two-, three-, or four-part round, with each new part beginning when the preceding part has finished the first line.

Whether the Weather

Whether the weather be fine, or
   whether the weather be not;
Whether the weather be cold, or
   whether the weather be hot;
Whatever the weather,
We'll weather the weather,
Whether we like it or not.

"Where O Where?" can be recited as a round or with accompaniments.

Where O Where?

I would I were where I would be
Then would I be where I am not;
For where I am I would not be,
And where I would be I cannot.

Accompaniment
Am I here? Am I there?
Am I really anywhere?
I am here! I am there!
I am really everywhere!

"Chuckling Chickens" works very well either as a round, with accompaniments, or as a round with accompaniments. For a simple round, start the second group after the first group has completed the first two lines. A more complicated round can have the new group after the first group has completed the first line.

Chuckling Chickens
Molly de Havas

Come watch the chuckling chickens
    as they search for things to eat,
They chirp and chatter cheerily
    and scratch about their feet.
From garden patch and wayside ditch–
    as much as they can catch–
They eat, and then each other chase
    a choicer bit to snatch.

Possible Accompaniments:
1. Brawk; brawk-brawk-brawk; brawk; brawk-brawk-brawk.
2. Pick a little, peck a little, pick a little, peck a little,
   Pick, pick, pick—got to peck a little bit.

At the end of the poem, a child can crow like a rooster.

Most of the speech exercises below can be done as rounds. Those with the same rhythm and number of lines could also be combined into quodlibets. A quodlibet is a musical composition that combines several different melodies either concurrently or as a round. For instance, "Row, Row, Row Your Boat" can be combined with "Frère Jacques" and/or with "Three Blind Mice" because these tunes have a similar rhythmic structure and their melodies blend harmoniously.

A speech quodlibet combines different poems concurrently or as a round. For instance "Cheap Sea Trips" can be combined with "Glue Gun Glue" to create a rich texture. These poems can also be done as rounds, with one group starting with one poem and the other group with the other. The second time through, they switch poems.

A Selection of Speech Rounds and Quodlibets

Cheap Sea Trips

I do like cheap sea trips
Cheap sea trips on ships.
I like to be on the deep blue sea
When the ship she rolls and dips

Glue Gun Glue

Go and get the glue gun glue
Glue gun glue to use
For glue gun glue must get quite hot
For glue gun glue to ooze.

Hewer Hugh

In Huron a hewer, Hugh Hughes,
Hewed yews of unusual hues.
Hugh Hughes used blue yews
To build sheds for his ewes;
So his ewes a blue-hued ewe-shed use.

Watch Out!

I have a new Swiss wristwatch.
So does my old pal Mitch.
If you switched his wristwatch
With my new Swiss wristwatch,
Could you tell which wristwatch was which?

Think of This!

I can think of six thin things,
Six thin things, can you?
Yes, I can think of six thin things,
And of six thick things too.

Pop's Bottles

Pop bottles bottles in pop bottle shops
The bottles Pop bottles poor Pop sometimes drops
When Pop drops the bottles, the pop-bottles plop
When pop-bottles topple, then poor Pop mops slop.

Bug Blood

Big black bugs bleed blue black blood,
But baby black bugs bleed blue.
Don't squish the big bugs or you'll get
Some blue black blood on you.

Who Drew What?

Drew and Lou drew drawings,
They both drew nicely... but...
Drew drew what Lou drew
And Lou drew what Drew drew
So nobody knew who drew what!

The Thief

Out of his hole to steal he stole
A bag of chink he chunk.
And many a wicked smile he smole
And many a wink he wunk.

Slippery Snakes

Swiftly slide the slippery snakes,
See them slither by,
Softly over stock and stone,
Slipping on the sly.

In your introduction to "The Bear and the Boar" make sure that students can differentiate the homophones. This poem could be used as an articulation exercise or as a breath control challenge by reciting it ever more rapidly.

The Bear and the Boar

Once upon a barren moor
There dwelt a bear, also a boar;
The bear could not bear the boar,
The boar thought the bear a bore.
At last the boar could bear no more
The bear that bored him on the moor,
And so one morn he bored the bear;
That bear will bore the boar no more.

Theophilus Thistledown

Theophilus Thistledown,
The successful thistle sifter,
In sifting a sieve
Of unsifted thistles
Stuck three thousand thistles
Through the thick of his thumb.

If Theophilus Thistledown,
The successful thistle sifter,
Stuck three thousand thistles
Through the thick of his thumb,
See that thou,
When sifting thistles,
Stick not the thistles
Through the thick of thy thumb!

Many fifth graders enjoy poems like these Willie poems because of their macabre nature.

Willie Poems

Willie's whistle wouldn't whistle
So away the thing he threw.
Then that whistle whistled briskly
As away it gaily flew.

In the family drinking well
Willie pushed his sister Nell.
She's there yet, because it kilt her
Now we'll have to buy a filter.

Willie with a thirst for gore,
Nailed the baby to the door.
Mother said, with humor quaint:
"Careful, Will, don't scratch the paint."

Willie poisoned Auntie's tea.
Auntie died in agony.
Uncle came and looked quite vexed.
"Really, Will," said he, "What next?"

Willie found some dynamite,
Couldn't understand it quite.
Curiosity never pays;
It rained Willie seven days.

"Shame on Sam" can be done as an articulation or breath control exercise by increasing the speed. Check that as the students begin to speak more quickly, they still enunciate clearly.

Shame on Sam
adapted by Roberto Trostli

It's a shame, Sam,
They're the same, Sam,
And a shame it is
To say shame, Sam.

Shame to say, Sam,
They're the same, Sam,
And a shame it is—
Don't you say, Sam?

Sam's Swimming
adapted by Roberto Trostli

Swim, Sam, swim!
Show them you're some swimmer.
I see six sharks come seeking snacks,
So swim, Sam, swim!

Sam swam well—
I've never seen such swimming!
The six sharks chased him for a spell
And swam away a-grinning.

TONGUE TWISTERS

Tongue twisters can be used as warm-ups for recitations or as speech exercises that focus on a sound or set of sounds. Because students learn most tongue twisters quickly, it's important to vary how we work with them. Once students can say a tongue twister fluently, variations can also serve as concentration exercises.

Tongue Twister Variations

1. Recite the tongue twister and have the students highlight the major sound by exaggerating it and saying it louder than the other sounds. For instance:
    The **B**leak **B**reeze **B**lights the **B**right **B**room **B**lossom.

2. Leave out the major sound. For instance:
    The _leak _reeze _lights the _right _room _lossom.

3. Turn the tongue twister into a progressive exercise by adding the next word each time. For instance:

> The
> The bleak
> The bleak breeze
> The bleak breeze blights
> The bleak breeze blights the
> The bleak breeze blights the bright
> The bleak breeze blights the bright broom
> The bleak breeze blights the bright broom blossom

As a variation, different groups of students can be called on to say the next line so that those not speaking listen carefully and inwardly participate in the exercise. It is nice to have the whole class say the entire tongue twister as a finale.

4. Move the tongue twister around the room by having the next child in the row say the next word. The goal is for the tongue twister to flow as smoothly as if one person was saying it. Once the students can do this fluently, point to students at random so that they have to stay ready to say the next word. This exercises requires students to continue to say the tongue twister inwardly even if they only have the chance to say one or two words out loud.

5. Turn the tongue twister into a progressive exercise by adding a new word backwards. For instance:

> blossom
> broom blossom
> bright broom blossom
> the bright broom blossom
> blights the bright broom blossom
> breeze blights the bright broom blossom
> bleak breeze blights the bright broom blossom
> The bleak breeze blights the bright broom blossom

Again, different groups of students can be called on to say the next line so that those not speaking listen carefully and inwardly participate in the exercise. It is nice to have the whole class say the entire tongue twister as a finale.

6. Recite the tongue twister in reverse order. Depending on its length and complexity, this can be extremely difficult, but it is good to challenge the students' memories.

> The bleak breeze blights the bright broom blossom
> Blossom broom bright the blights breeze bleak the

After saying the tongue twister in reverse order several times, some students will be able to say it fluently without much effort.

A Selection of Tongue Twisters[2]

A box of biscuits; a box of mixed biscuits; and a biscuit mixer.

The bleak breeze blights the bright broom blossom.

Can Kitty cuddle Clara's kitten?

Chilly chili will become more chilly if you stir chilly chili willy-nilly.

Cheek, chin, cheek, chin, cheek, chin, nose,
Cheek, chin, cheek, chin, cheek, chin, toes.

White cats, black cats, slick cats, slack cats;
Rough cats, sleek cats, fierce cats, meek cats:
So many kinds of kitty-cats all seated in a row,
Cooped in cozy cages for the kitty-cat show.

Dashing dangerously down the dale dainty, Dinah dashed dizzily past Dorothy.

Dashing Daniel defied David to deliver Dora from the dawning danger.

Three fiddling pigs sat in a pit and fiddled;
Fiddle, piggy, fiddle, piggy, fiddle, piggy.

Fifteen frightened fluffy fowls fly foolishly through the farmyard.

A fine field of wheat; a field of fine wheat

Hear the happy hunter's horn
High over hill and hedge and thorn.

Ike ships ice chips in ice chip ships.
The chips he ships are ice chips, I'm sure.

Jangling our jam-jars and jumping for joy,
Far from the village a journey we make,
Ranging the generous hedges and fields,
Juicy, jet blackberries gently to take.

Many an anemone sees an enemy anemone.

---

[2] Additional tongue twisters can be found at the ends of the chapters for 6th, 7th, and 8th grades.

Men munch much mush.
Women munch much mush.
Many men and women munch much mush.

Pat's pa Pete poked a pea patch to pick a peck of peas to feed the poor pink pig in the pine pole pen.

Pure food for poor mules. Pure food for poor mules. Pure food for poor mules.

Put the cut pumpkin in a pipkin.

A truly rural frugal ruler's mural

Shave a cedar shingle thin.

She saw the shiny soapy suds sailing down the shallow sink.

Sheep shouldn't sleep in a shack; sheep should sleep in a shed.

Shelly served chilly chili to silly Sally.
Serving chilly chili to silly Sally, Shelly said,
"Stir it soundly, silly!"

If silly Sally will shilly shally
Shall silly Willy willy nilly shilly shally too?

Snow and ice and silvered hedges,
Sleet and slush and slides and sledges.

The city sweep shook his sooty sheet in the city street.

The rain ceaseth and suffices us.

The school scold sold the school coal scuttle.

Tim, the thin twin tinsmith;
Slim, the thin tinsmith's twin.

Tim's black ticktock clock ticks,
But Tom's black ticktock clock clicks.

These are these and those are those as long as we go hither,
But these are those and those are these as soon as we are thither.

Recitation in Sixth Grade

Sixth graders are going through an important developmental stage: the 12th-year change. Poised between childhood and adolescence, they still identify strongly with their friends, but they are beginning to feel increasingly independent, self-conscious, and insecure. Most sixth graders have not yet embarked on that lonely quest for identity that will occur in the coming years, but they are beginning to have hints of what it means to be an individual. Their study of history and literature depicts positive and negative characters and choices, which helps them develop their sense of self.

The recitation curriculum for sixth grade includes selections from history, serious and humorous poems, speech exercises, and tongue twisters. The selections from history include excerpts in Latin, Old English, and Middle English that are done in the original languages. This allows students to get a first-hand experience of the cultures they are studying. The serious and humorous poems speak to the sixth graders' affinity for contrast and polarities; and the speech exercises and tongue twisters challenge them to refine their enunciation and to gain better breath control.

Morning Exercises in sixth grade no longer need to be coordinated with the Main Lesson blocks, though I encourage that you to continue this practice when practicable. Working on Morning Exercises for about month at a time helps students master the selections and gives them an opportunity to eventually recite the works on their own to demonstrate their mastery. Works that do not need to be worked on for the whole block can be replaced by new selections.

Before beginning to work on a recitation, you should introduce it. Recitations about curricular subjects need no introduction because the Main Lesson presentation will have provided the context. For all other selections, introductions should include the title and the author of the work, and, if you wish, something about the author's life and the work's background and context.

Next you should provide a brief summary of the work and speak about the important themes, people, or events. If the form and style of the work are important, they should be mentioned, and if any literary devices are used, they should be highlighted. If the work is in a language other than English, your introduction should provide enough of a foundation for students to appreciate the correspondence between the original and the translation.

Introductions to works with particularly meaningful themes, characters, or events should include your comments. I encourage you to express your opinion freely because your students will learn a great deal, not only about the recitation, but about you. Introductions to important works can also include a class discussion that explores the work's importance and relevance. These discussions strengthen the class community as the students get to know each other better, and they deepen our bond with our students as we express what we think and believe.

What has been described all occurs *before* students hear the work for the first time. This approach may seem counter-intuitive because we typically discuss and analyze a work *after* we have heard it. But this approach appeals to the students' feelings, especially to their curiosity and interest. Then when they hear the work for the first time, students will connect with the work more completely, understand more it deeply, and appreciate it more fully.

If you wish to learn more about this novel approach, please refer to Discussion 6 of *Discussions with Teachers*, where Rudolf Steiner demonstrated how a teacher might introduce a fable or a poem. If you are new to this method, I encourage you to try it. Although you may feel a bit awkward at first, I believe that you will quickly experience how well it works.

In previous years, many recitations were recited in unison or in groups. In sixth grade, individual voices should be heard, and students need to feel responsible for holding their part among the other parts. Recitations should therefore be divided among groups of students or distributed among individuals. Students have to learn that when a group recites together, they need to moderate their personal interpretation and blend with the group. When students recite on their own, they should be encouraged to express their individual approach to the selection. Suggestions for how to work with quodlibets may be found on pages 34–36, 67–68, 103–105, and 152.

Sixth graders enjoy tongue twisters because they challenge their memories, refine their enunciation, and help them develop greater agility in their speech. Because sixth graders master tongue twisters so quickly, they should be recited with variations and not be worked on too long lest they become stale. Detailed instructions about various ways to work with tongue twisters may be found on pages 38–41, 69–75, 105–109, and 152–154.

Morning Exercises help students to leave their lives outside of school aside and focus on what they are learning and doing at school. Although Morning Exercises are important, they should not exceed about 30 minutes per day. When we spend too much time on them, students can become less attentive and responsive and may have difficulty concentrating on their work. A class benefits greatly from the Morning Exercises, but we need to remember that they are only a preparation for—not a major component of—the Main Lesson.

YEARLY VERSES

Verses that are recited throughout the year have a special place in the speech curriculum. The daily repetition of these verses imprints them in the students' hearts and affirms their ideals.

A typical sixth-grade Main Lesson begins with announcements, class housekeeping, and perhaps a brief check-in. All of these should precede the recitation of the Morning Verse so that the verse can serve as a formal beginning to the Main Lesson. I encourage the upper grades in your school to use the same version of the Morning Verse because this strengthens the sense of community among the students. I have therefore not included versions of the Morning Verse because it is important for each school to choose the one they prefer.

Throughout the years, my classes recited the following verses: "There Lives in Me an Image," at the end of the Morning Exercises, "May Wisdom Shine through Me," at the end of the Main Lesson, and "At the Ringing of the Bells" at the end of the day.

Angelus Silesius (1624–1677) was the name that Johann Scheffler adopted when he became a Catholic priest. He composed many religious poems that expressed his mystical beliefs.

There Lives in Me an Image
Angelus Silesius

There lives in me an image,
Of all that I should be;
Until I have become it,
My heart is never free.

May Wisdom Shine through Me
Rudolf Steiner

May wisdom shine through me,
May love glow within me,
May strength permeate me,
That in me may arise
A helper of humankind,
A server of holy things,
Selfless and true.

At the Ringing of the Bells
Rudolf Steiner

To wonder at beauty,
Stand guard over truth,
Look up to the noble,
Decide for the good—
Leads us on our journey
To goals for our life:
To right in our doing;
To peace in our feeling;
To light in our thought.
And teaches us trust
In the guidance of God;
In all that there is—
In the world-wide All,
In the soul's deep soil.

RECITATIONS FROM HISTORY

The history curriculum in sixth grade provides many possibilities for poetry and prose recitations. These can be worked on throughout the year, not only during history Main Lesson blocks.

If students at your school learn Latin, this will greatly enrich their study of Roman history. If they don't, I suggest that they learn "O Roma Nobilis" or the beginning of the Aeneid in Latin to allow them to experience a little bit of the language. You will need to decide whether you want the students to learn the Latin first without translating it, and then later begin to show the correspondences between the Latin words and their English equivalents, or whether you want to include the translation in your introduction. Whichever you choose, by the time they have learned the recitation, the students should know what each of the Latin words means.

"O Roma Nobilis" derives from the 10th century. It was sung by pilgrims when they arrived at the tombs of St. Peter and St. Paul, and it has been set to music by several modern composers. Although sixth graders are more self-conscious about accompanying a recitation with gestures, I recommend doing so with this poem.

O Roma Nobilis

O Roma nobilis!
Orbis et domina
Omnium urbium
Excellentissima.
Salutem dicimus
Tibi per omnia.
Te benedicimus
Salve per saecula.

O noble Rome,
Mistress of the world.
Most excellent
Of all cities.
For all we salute thee
We bless thee:
Hail for all ages!

Your study of Roman history might begin with a telling of *The Aeneid*, because it bridges Greek and Roman history. If you tell this story, consider teaching the students the opening lines of Vergil's epic so that they can experience the lofty language and the use of the hexameter.

Opening Lines of **The Aeneid**
Vergil

Arma virumque cano, Troiae qui primus ab oris
Italiam, fato profugus, Laviniaque venit
litora, multum ille et terris iactatus et alto
vi superum saevae memorem Iunonis ob iram;
multa quoque et bello passus, dum conderet urbem,
inferretque deos Latio, genus unde Latinum,
Albanique patres, atque altae moenia Romae.

Here are two translations—classic translated by John Dryden (1631–1700) and a contemporary translation by Shadi Bartch-Zimmer (1966–), professor of Classics at the University of Chicago.

Opening Lines of Vergil's Aeneid
translated by John Dryden

Arms and the man I sing, who, forced by fate
And haughty Juno's unrelenting hate,
Expelled and exiled, left the Trojan shore.
Long labors, both by sea and land, he bore;
And in the doubtful war, before he won
The Latin realm and built the destined town,
His banished gods restored to rights divine,
And settled sure succession in his line;
From whence the race of Alban fathers come,
And the long glories of majestic Rome.

Opening Lines of Vergil's Aeneid
translated by Shadi Bartch-Zimmer

My song is of war and a man: a refugee by fate,
the first from Troy to Italy's Lavinian shores,
battered much on land and sea by blows from gods
obliging brutal Juno's unforgetting rage;
he suffered much in war as well, all to plant
his town and gods in Latium. From here would rise
the Latin race, the Alban lords, and Rome's high walls.

Hannibal is one of the most interesting characters that students encounter in the sixth-grade history curriculum. If you have told the story of his army's epic crossing of the Alps, this selection from Juvenal needs no introduction. If you did not describe Hannibal's epic journey, you might mention how the Alpine rocks became friable when they were heated and doused with vinegar, and you might tell the students that acid decomposes limestone (a topic that will be explored in seventh grade chemistry.) Although Juvenal intended this passage to be satirical, it can be recited with respect and admiration.

Hannibal
Juvenal

This is the man for whom Africa
Was too small a continent,
Though it stretched from the shores of Morocco
East to the steamy Nile.

Now Spain swells his empire;
Now he surmounts the Pyrenees;
Nature sets in his path
High mountain passes, blizzards of snow;
But he splits the very rocks asunder,
Moves mountains with vinegar.
Now Italy is his, but still he forces on.
"We have accomplished nothing," he cries,
"Till we have stormed the gates of Rome;
Till our Carthaginian standard
Is set in the city's heart!"

Julius Caesar is a major figure in Roman history. I recommend that you have your students read a section of Shakespeare's "Julius Caesar," and that you have them learn at least one of the speeches below. In your introduction, you might speak a bit about Shakespeare's life (1564–1616) and his profound influence on the development of the English language. Students benefit from a description of when the speeches occur in the play and which characters are speaking. It will be useful to paraphrase the selection before reading it for the first time so that the students understand most of it.

Selections from Julius Caesar
William Shakespeare

Why, man, he doth bestride the narrow world
Like a Colossus, and we petty men
Walk under his huge legs and peep about
To find ourselves dishonourable graves.
Men at some time are masters of their fates:
The fault, dear Brutus, is not in our stars,
But in ourselves, that we are underlings.
...

I could be well moved, if I were as you;
If I could pray to move, prayers would move me:
But I am constant as the Northern Star,
Of whose true-fixed and resting quality
There is no fellow in the firmament.
The skies are painted with unnumb'red sparks,
They are all fire, and every one doth shine;
But there's but one in all doth hold his place.
So in the world: 'tis furnished well with men,
And men are flesh and blood and apprehensive.
Yet in their number I do know but one
That unassailable holds on his rank,
Unshaked of motion; and that I am he.

Brutus's funeral oration is one of Shakespeare's most famous speeches. If you decide not to have your students learn it as a recitation, you might do it as a dramatic reading. In your introduction, you might mention Shakespeare's use of irony in the repeated phrase, "So are they all honorable men."

> Friends, Romans, countrymen, lend me your ears;
> I come to bury Caesar, not to praise him.
> The evil that men do lives after them;
> The good is oft interred with their bones;
> So let it be with Caesar. The noble Brutus
> Hath told you Caesar was ambitious:
> If it were so, it was a grievous fault,
> And grievously hath Caesar answer'd it.
> Here, under leave of Brutus and the rest–
> For Brutus is an honorable man;
> So are they all, all honorable men–
> Come I to speak in Caesar's funeral.
> He was my friend, faithful and just to me:
> But Brutus says he was ambitious;
> And Brutus is an honorable man.
> He hath brought many captives home to Rome
> Whose ransoms did the general coffers fill:
> Did this in Caesar seem ambitious?
> When that the poor have cried, Caesar hath wept:
> Ambition should be made of sterner stuff:
> Yet Brutus says he was ambitious;
> And Brutus is an honorable man.
> You all did see that on the Lupercal
> I thrice presented him a kingly crown,
> Which he did thrice refuse: was this ambition?
> Yet Brutus says he was ambitious;
> And, sure, he is an honorable man.
> I speak not to disprove what Brutus spoke,
> But here I am to speak what I do know.
> You all did love him once, not without cause:
> What cause withholds you then, to mourn for him?
> O judgment! thou art fled to brutish beasts,
> And men have lost their reason. Bear with me;
> My heart is in the coffin there with Caesar,
> And I must pause till it come back to me.

The study of Medieval History might include the Norse depredations of England and coastal Europe, which set the stage for the Norman Conquest. The old English poem, "The Battle of Maldon," provides a vivid example of the plight of the English during a Viking attack. Students are often impressed by the power of Old English poetry, with its strong rhythm and alliteration. Refer to online resources to learn the correct pronunciation.

In your introduction, you might prepare the students by describing the situation, the characters, and the events. When you work on a selection, review the correspondences between the Old English and the Modern English words so that the students understand what they are saying.

The Battle of Maldon (excerpt)

Wōdon þā wælwulfas (for wætere ne murnon),
wīċinga werod west ofer Pantan,
ofer scīr wæter scyldas wēgon,
lidmen tō lande linde bæron.

Strode then the slaughter wolves, bold through the water,
The troop of the pirates, west over Panta;
Over bright water, their shields they bore
Bearing their lindens, seamen to shore.

Byrhtwold maþelode, bord hafenode
(se wæs eald ġenēat), æsc ācwehte;
hē ful baldlīċe beornas lærde:
"Hiġe sceal þē heardra, heorte þē cēnre,
mōd sceal þē māre þē ūre mæġen lætlað.
Hēr līð ūre ealdor eall forhēawen
gōd on grēote. Ā mæġ gnornian
se ðe nū fram þisum wīġplegan wendan þenċeð.

Byrhtwold spoke, raised his shield—
he was an old retainer—shook his ash-spear;
full boldly he taught warriors:
"Thought must be the harder, heart be the keener,
mind must be the greater,
while our strength lessens.
Here lies our prince, all forehewn,
a good man on the ground.
Always may mourn
he who from this war-play
now thinks to turn."

I recommend including the life and work of Chaucer in your study of Medieval history and teaching your students the Prologue to *The Canterbury Tales*—the most famous passage in Middle English.

Geoffrey Chaucer (ca. 1340–1400) was the foremost medieval English poet, and his works helped transform the English language. Your introduction might illuminate the correspondences between the Middle English words and their modern equivalents. When your students practice the recitation, review the unfamiliar words so that they can recite with understanding. The correct pronunciation can be learned from online sources.

The Canterbury Tales *(excerpt from the Prologue)*
Geoffrey Chaucer

Whan that Aprill with his shoures soote
The droghte of March hath perced to the roote,
And bathed every veyne in swich licour
Of which vertu engendred is the flour;
Whan Zephirus eek with his sweete breeth
Inspired hath in every holt and heeth
The tendre croppes, and the yonge sonne
Hath in the Ram his half cours yronne,
And smale foweles maken melodye,
That slepen al the night with open eye
(So priketh hem Nature in hir corages);
Than longen folk to goon on pilgrimages,
And palmeres for to seken straunge strondes,
To ferne halwes, kowthe in sondry londes;
And specially from every shires ende
Of Engelonde to Caunterbury they wende,
The hooly blisful martir for to seke,
That hem hath holpen whan that they were seke.

"The Blacksmiths," a poem from the 14th century, captures the sounds of a Medieval industrial smithy. If you have already told the students about the Medieval guilds, the content of the poem needs little introduction. If not, you might describe the ironworkers' guilds and the smiths' working conditions. Prepare the students for the recitation by reminding them about alliteration and by giving them some examples of onomatopoeia from the original Middle English.

The Blacksmiths

    Swart smirched smiths, smattered with smoke
    Drive me to death with din of their dents,
    Such noise on nights ne'er heard man never,
    Such clashing of cries and clattering of knocks.
    The craftsmen clamour for coal, coal, coal!
    And blow their bellows their brains to burst.
    They jostle and jangle, they jape and they jest.
    They groove and they grind and they grumble together,
    Hot with the heaving of heated hammers.
    Of thick bull's hide are their branded aprons,
    Their shanks are shod 'gainst shooting sparks.
    Huge hammers they have and hard to handle,
    Stark strokes strike they on the steeled stock.
    "Well wrought, well wrought, well wrought,"
    Might daunt the devil
    Such life they lead,
    All armourers, founders, forgemen,
    Christ save them!

As a special challenge, you can use the original poem—or sections of it—as a speech exercise. Guidance for pronunciation can be found online.

    Swarte smekyd smethes, smateryd wyth smoke,
    Dryue me to deth wyth den of here dyntes.
    Swech noys on nyghtes ne herd men neuer.
    What knauene cry and clateryng of knockes!
    The cammede kongons cryen after "col, col!"
    And blowen here bellewys, that al here brayn brestes.
    "Huf, puf!" seyth that on; "haf, paf!" that other.
    Thei spytten and spraulyn and spellyn many spelles.
    Thei gnauen and gnacchen, thei gronys togydere
    And holdyn hem hote wyth here hard hamers.
    Of a bole hyde ben here barm-fellys.
    Here schankes ben schakeled for the fere-flunderys.
    Heuy hamerys thei han, that hard ben handled.
    Stark strokes thei stryken on a stelyd stokke.
    Lus, bus! las, das! rowtyn be rowe.
    Swech dolful a dreme the deuyl it todryue!
    The mayster longith a lityl, and lascheth a lesse,
    Twyneth hem tweyn, and towchith a treble.
    Tik, tak! hic, hac! tiket, taket! tyk, tak!
    Lus, bus! lus, das! Swych lyf thei ledyn,
    Alle clothemerys, Cryst hem gyue sorwe!
    May no man for brenwaterys on nyght han hys rest.

SERIOUS POEMS

Sixth graders can be reserved and thoughtful, so they benefit from learning some poems that have serious themes.

Kalidasa was a Classical Sanskrit author who is often considered ancient India's greatest poet and playwright. He lived during the Gupta empire, which lasted from the early fourth to the late 6th century CE.

Salutation to the Dawn
Kalidasa

Look to this day!
For it is life, the very life of life.
In its brief course
Lie all the verities and realities of your existence:
The bliss of growth;
The glory of action;
The splendor of beauty;
For yesterday is but a dream,
And tomorrow only a vision;
But today well lived makes every yesterday
A dream of happiness
And every tomorrow a vision of hope.
Look well, therefore, to this day!
Such is the salutation of the dawn.

Maltbie Davenport Babcock (1858–1901) was a noted American clergyman, who is best known for writing the well-known hymn "This is My Father's World." In your introduction, you might speak about the very direct way that he addresses his audience. Then you can have your students discuss whether this approach is effective. You might also draw their attention to the power of repetition and the poem's rhyme scheme.

Be Strong!
Maltbie Davenport Babcock

Be strong!
We are not here to play, to dream, to drift;
We have hard work to do, and loads to lift;
Shun not the struggle—face it; 'tis god's gift.

Be strong!
Say not,"The days are evil. Who's to blame?"
And fold the hands and acquiesce—oh shame!
Stand up, speak out, and bravely, in God's name.

Be strong!
It matters not how deep entrenched the wrong;
How hard the battle goes, the day how long;
Faint not—fight not! Tomorrow comes the song.

In your introduction to this poem, mention that the Egyptian pyramids and the sphinx were symbols of power; this will prepare students to appreciate the decay conveyed by this poem. You might also point out that the poem includes perspectives from four people: the narrator, the traveler, the architect, and Ozymandias. In the recitation, the words "stretch far away" can be drawn out to evoke the far horizons of space and time.

Percy Bysshe Shelley (1792–1822) lived a tumultuous life and died in a boating accident at age 29. He was not well-known during his lifetime, but his works greatly influenced later generations of writers.

Ozymandias of Egypt
Percy Bysshe Shelley

I met a traveler from an antique land
Who said: Two vast and trunkless legs of stone
Stand in the desert... Near them on the sand
Half sunk, a shattered visage lies, whose frown,
And wrinkled lip, and sneer of cold command,
Tell that its sculptor well those passions read
Which yet survive, stamped on these lifeless things,
The hand that mock'd them and the heart that fed:
And on the pedestal these words appear:
"My name is Ozymandias, king of kings:
Look on my works, ye Mighty, and despair!"
Nothing beside remains. Round the decay
Of that colossal wreck, boundless and bare,
The lone and level sands stretch far away.

Emily Dickinson (1830–1886) lived in Amherst, MA, and rarely left the family homestead. She was a prolific poet, but most of her poems were not known during her lifetime because she hid them away in her home. "Blazing in Gold" is a typical Emily Dickinson poem that has vivid images and directness. It is an implied riddle, so as the students learn it, ask them who they think "the juggler of the day" is.

Blazing in Gold and Quenching in Purple
Emily Dickinson

Blazing in gold and quenching in purple,
Leaping like leopards to the sky,
Then at the feet of the old horizon
Laying her spotted face, to die;
Stooping as low as the kitchen window,
Touching the roof and tinting the barn,
Kissing her bonnet to the meadow,—
And the juggler of day is gone!

Walter de la Mare (1873–1956) was an English author, who wrote many poems for children. This poem could be recited during October because of Hallowe'en. It is especially suitable for sixth grade because the students will be studying astronomy during the year. In your introduction you might review the constellations mentioned in the poem.

The Ride-by-Nights
Walter de la Mare

Up on their brooms the Witches stream,
Crooked and black in the crescent's gleam,
One foot high, and one foot low,
Bearded, cloaked, and cowled, they go.
'Neath Charlie's Wane they twitter and tweet,
And away they swarm 'neath the Dragon's feet,
With a whoop and a flutter they swing and sway,
And surge pell-mell down the Milky Way.
Between the legs of the glittering Chair
They hover and squeak in the empty air.
Then round they swoop past the glimmering Lion
To where Sirius barks behind huge Orion;
Up, then, and over to wheel amain
Under the silver, and home again.

Elizabeth Coatsworth (1893–1986) was a writer of fiction and poetry for adults and children. She won the Newbery Medal for her novel, *The Cat Who Went to Heaven*. In your introduction to this poem, you might speak with your students what effect is achieved by having the poem narrated by the camels who brought the three kings to Bethlehem.

Song of the Camels
Elizabeth Jane Coatsworth

Not born to the forest are we,
Not born to the plain,
To the grass and the shadowing tree
And the splashing of rain.
Only the sand we know
And the cloudless sky.
The mirage and the deep-sunk well
And the stars on high.

To the sound of our bells we came
With huge soft stride,
Kings riding upon our backs,
Slaves at our side.
Out of the east drawn on
By a dream and a star,
Seeking the hills and the groves
Where the fixed towns are.

Our goal was no palace gate,
No temple of old,
But a child on his mother's lap
In the cloudy cold.
The olives were windy and white,
Dust swirled through the town,
As all in their royal robes
Our masters knelt down.

Robert Frost (1874–1963) was one of the best-known American poets of his time. Like many of his poems, "Stopping by Woods on a Snowy Evening" is deceptively simple but hints at deeper questions. In your introduction, you might review the situation of the traveler and the horse and have your students consider the question: "What kind of promises must the poet keep before he sleeps?" Once the students have learned the poem, I recommend analyzing the rhyme scheme that binds the stanzas together.

Stopping by Woods on a Snowy Evening
Robert Frost

Whose woods these are I think I know.
His house is in the village, though;
He will not see me stopping here
To watch his woods fill up with snow.

My little horse must think it queer
To stop without a farmhouse near
Between the woods and frozen lake
The darkest evening of the year.

He gives his harness bell a shake
To ask if there is some mistake.
The only other sound's the sweep
Of easy wind and downy flake.

The woods are lovely, dark, and deep.
But I have promises to keep,
And miles to go before I sleep,
And miles to go before I sleep.

William Wordsworth (1770–1850) was one of the foremost English Romantic poets. Wordsworth saw not only beauty but meaning in nature, and he tried to convey this through the images in poems like "Daffodils." In your introduction, help the students imagine the scene that Wordsworth portrays and ask them to describe the feelings that such a scene might evoke. As you work on this recitation, make sure that the students understand the meaning of the unfamiliar words like 'jocund,' 'sprightly,' or 'pensive,' and tell them that in Wordsworth's day, the word 'gay' meant 'lighthearted' or 'carefree.'

Daffodils
William Wordsworth

I wandered lonely as a cloud
    That floats on high o'er vales and hills,
When all at once I saw a crowd,
    A host, of golden daffodils:
Beside the lake, beneath the trees,
    Fluttering and dancing in the breeze.

Continuous as the stars that shine
   And twinkle on the Milky Way,
They stretched in never-ending line
   Along the margin of a bay:
Ten thousand saw I at a glance,
   Tossing their heads in sprightly dance.

The waves beside them dance, but they
   Outdid the sparkling waves in glee:
A poet could not but be gay,
   In such a jocund company;
I gazed—and gazed—but little thought
   What wealth the show to me had brought;

For oft, when on my couch I lie
   In vacant or in pensive mood,
They flash upon that inward eye
   Which is the bliss of solitude;
And then my heart with pleasure fills,
   And dances with the daffodils.

Maya Angelou (1928–2014) was a prolific American essayist, novelist, playwright and poet. She was active in the civil rights movement during the time of Dr. Martin Luther King Jr. and Malcolm X. In your introduction you might have the students list what things they think engender fear in young children and compare them with Maya Angelou's list. You might also consider how Maya Angelou uses repetition to reinforce the poem's message.

Life Doesn't Frighten Me
Maya Angelou

Shadows on the wall
Noises down the hall
Life doesn't frighten me at all

Bad dogs barking loud
Big ghosts in a cloud
Life doesn't frighten me at all

Mean old Mother Goose
Lions on the loose
They don't frighten me at all

Dragons breathing flame
On my counterpane
That doesn't frighten me at all.

I go boo
Make them shoo
I make fun
Way they run
I won't cry
So they fly
I just smile
They go wild

Life doesn't frighten me at all.

Tough guys fight
All alone at night
Life doesn't frighten me at all.

Panthers in the park
Strangers in the dark
No, they don't frighten me at all.

That new classroom where
Boys all pull my hair
(Kissy little girls
With their hair in curls)
They don't frighten me at all.

Don't show me frogs and snakes
And listen for my scream,
If I'm afraid at all
It's only in my dreams.

I've got a magic charm
That I keep up my sleeve
I can walk the ocean floor
And never have to breathe.

Life doesn't frighten me at all
Not at all
Not at all.

Life doesn't frighten me at all.

HUMOROUS POEMS

Sixth graders love humor of every sort: melodrama, eccentric characters, unusual plot twists, and surprise endings. Hillaire Belloc (1870–1953) was an orator, writer, and historian. His humorous poems about children are easy to memorize because of their rhythm and rhyme. Students who like this kind of light verse can be encouraged to read other poems by Hillaire Belloc. In your introduction to "A Cautionary Tale," you might speak about the poet's use of hyperbole and satire to make his point. Once the students have learned the poem, it can be dramatized—or over-dramatized—at an assembly.

A Cautionary Tale
Hillaire Belloc

There was a Boy whose name was Jim;
His friends were very good to him.
They gave him Tea, and Cakes, and Jam,
And slices of delicious Ham,
And Chocolates with pink inside,
And little Tricycles to ride,
And read him Stories through and through,
And even took him to the Zoo—
But there it was the dreadful Fate
Befell him, which I now relate.
You know—at least you ought to know,
For I have often told you so—
That Children never are allowed
To leave their Nurses in a Crowd;
Now this was Jim's especial Foible,
He ran away when he was able,
And on this inauspicious day
He slipped his hand and ran away!
He hadn't gone a yard when—Bang!
With open Jaws, a Lion sprang,
And hungrily began to eat
The Boy: beginning at his feet.
Now just imagine how it feels
When first your toes and then your heels,
And then by gradual degrees,
Your shins and ankles, calves and knees,
Are slowly eaten, bit by bit.
No wonder Jim detested it!
No wonder that he shouted"Hi!"
The Honest Keeper heard his cry,
Though very fat, he almost ran
To help the little gentleman.

"Ponto!" he ordered as he came
(For Ponto was the Lion's name),
"Ponto!" he cried, with angry Frown.
"Let go, Sir! Down, Sir! Put it down!"
The Lion made a sudden Stop,
He let the Dainty Morsel drop,
And slunk reluctant to his Cage,
Snarling in disappointed Rage.
But when he bent him over Jim,
The Honest Keeper's Eyes were dim.
The Lion having reached his Head,
The Miserable Boy was dead!
When Nurse informed his Parents, they
Were more Concerned than I can say:
His mother, as She dried her eyes,
Said, "Well, it gives me no surprise,
He would not do as he was told!"
His Father, who was self-controlled,
Bade all the children round attend
To James' miserable end,
And always keep a-hold of Nurse
For fear of finding something worse.

Lewis Carroll, the pen name of Charles Lutwidge Dodgson (1832–1898), was an Oxford professor of mathematics. He is best known for *Alice's Adventures in Wonderland* and its sequel, *Through the Looking Glass*. In addition to "The Walrus and the Carpenter" he wrote several other humorous poems, including "The Hunting of the Snark," which some students may enjoy reading. Before reciting the poem to them for the first time, you might introduce the characters and give the students a sense of their temperaments and how Carroll conveys them. You might also show the students how the poet suspends the listeners' disbelief by making humorous comments about the characters and actions in the poem.

The Walrus and the Carpenter
Lewis Carroll

The sun was shining on the sea,
    Shining with all his might:
He did his very best to make
    The billows smooth and bright—
And this was odd, because it was
    The middle of the night.

The moon was shining sulkily
    Because she thought the sun
Had got no business to be there
    After the day was done—
"It's very rude of him," she said,
    "To come and spoil the fun!"

The sea was wet as wet could be,
    The sands were dry as dry,
You could not see a cloud because
    No cloud was in the sky:
No birds were flying overhead—
    There were no birds to fly.

The Walrus and the Carpenter
    Were walking close at hand:
They wept like anything to see
    Such quantities of sand:
"If this were only cleared away,"
    They said, "it would be grand!"

"If seven maids with seven mops
    Swept it for half a year,
Do you suppose," the Walrus said,
    "That they could get it clear?"
"I doubt it," said the Carpenter
    And shed a bitter tear.

"O Oysters come and walk with us!"
    The Walrus did beseech.
"A pleasant walk, a pleasant talk,
    Along the briny beach:
We cannot do with more than four,
    To give a hand to each."

The eldest Oyster looked at him
    But never a word he said:
The eldest Oyster winked his eye,
    And shook his heavy head—
Meaning to say he did not choose
    To leave the oyster-bed.

But four young Oysters hurried up,
    All eager for the treat:
Their coats were brushed, their faces washed,
    Their shoes were clean and neat—
And this was odd, because, you know,
    They hadn't any feet.

Four other oysters followed them,
    And yet another four;
And thick and fast they came at last,
    And more and more and more—
All hopping through the frothy waves,
    And scrambling to the shore.

The Walrus and the Carpenter
    Walked on a mile or so,
And then they rested on a rock
    Conveniently low:
And all the little Oysters stood
    And waited in a row.

"The time has come," the Walrus said,
    "To talk of many things:
Of shoes—and ships—and sealing wax—
    Of cabbages—and kings—
And why the sea is boiling hot—
    And whether pigs have wings."

"But wait a bit," the Oysters cried,
    "Before we have our chat:
For some of us are out of breath,
    And all of us are fat!"
"No hurry!" said the Carpenter,
    They thanked him much for that.

"A loaf of bread," the Walrus said,
    "Is what we chiefly need:
Pepper and vinegar besides
    Are very good indeed—
Now, if you're ready Oysters dear,
    We can begin to feed."

"But not on us!" the Oysters cried,
    Turning a little blue.
"After such kindness, that would be
    A dismal thing to do!"
"The night is fine," the Walrus said,
    "Do you admire the view?"

"It was so kind of you to come!
    And you are very nice!"
The Carpenter said nothing but
    "Cut us another slice.
I wish you were not quite so deaf—
    I've had to ask you twice."

"It seems a shame," the Walrus said,
   "To play them such a trick.
After we've brought them out so far,
   And made them trot so quick."
The Carpenter said nothing but
   "The butter's spread too thick!"

"I weep for you," the Walrus said:
   "I deeply sympathize."
With sobs and tears he sorted out
   Those of the largest size,
Holding his pocket handkerchief
   Before his streaming eyes.

"O Oysters," said the Carpenter,
   "You've had a pleasant run!
Shall we be trotting home again?"
   But answer came there none.
And this was scarcely odd because
   They'd eaten every one.

Ernest Lawrence Thayer (1863–1940) worked for two years as a humor columnist for the *San Francisco Chronicle* after graduating from Harvard, where he edited *The Harvard Lampoon*. He contributed many humorous articles and poems to the *Chronicle* including "Casey at the Bat," which quickly became one of the best-known pieces of American comic verse. This poem needs little introduction because it tells the story so clearly. When the students begin working on it, you might elucidate some of the slang words that are no longer used.

Casey at the Bat
Ernest Lawrence Thayer

The outlook wasn't brilliant for the Mudville nine that day;
The score stood four to two with but one inning more to play.
And then when Cooney died at first, and Barrows did the same,
A sickly silence fell upon the patrons of the game.

A straggling few got up to go in deep despair. The rest
Clung to that hope which springs eternal in the human breast;
They thought if only Casey could but get a whack at that—
We'd put up even money now with Casey at the bat.

But Flynn preceded Casey, as did also Jimmy Blake,
And the former was a lulu and the latter was a cake;
So upon that stricken multitude grim melancholy sat,
For there seemed but little chance of Casey's getting to the bat.

But Flynn let drive a single, to the wonderment of all,
And Blake, the much despised, tore the cover off the ball;
And when the dust had lifted, and men saw what had occurred,
There was Jimmy safe at second and Flynn a-hugging third.

Then from 5,000 throats and more there rose a lusty yell;
It rumbled through the valley, it rattled in the dell;
It knocked upon the mountain and recoiled upon the flat,
For Casey, mighty Casey, was advancing to the bat.

There was ease in Casey's manner as he stepped into his place;
There was pride in Casey's bearing and a smile on Casey's face.
And when, responding to the cheers, he lightly doffed his hat,
No stranger in the crowd could doubt 'twas Casey at the bat.

Ten thousand eyes were on him as he rubbed his hands with dirt;
Five thousand tongues applauded when he wiped them on his shirt.
Then while the writhing pitcher ground the ball into his hip,
Defiance gleamed in Casey's eye, a sneer curled Casey's lip.

And now the leather-covered sphere came hurtling through the air,
And Casey stood a-watching it in haughty grandeur there.
Close by the sturdy batsman the ball unheeded sped—
"That ain't my style," said Casey. "Strike one," the umpire said.

From the benches, black with people, there went up a muffled roar,
Like the beating of the storm-waves on a stern and distant shore.
"Kill him! Kill the umpire!" shouted some one on the stand;
And it's likely they'd have killed him had not Casey raised his hand.

With a smile of Christian charity great Casey's visage shone;
He stilled the rising tumult; he bade the game go on;
He signaled to the pitcher, and once more the spheroid flew;
But Casey still ignored it, and the umpire said, "Strike two."

"Fraud!" cried the maddened thousands, and echo answered fraud;
But one scornful look from Casey and the audience was awed.
They saw his face grow stern and cold, they saw his muscles strain,
And they knew that Casey wouldn't let that ball go by again.

The sneer is gone from Casey's lip, his teeth are clinched in hate;
He pounds with cruel violence his bat upon the plate.
And now the pitcher holds the ball, and now he lets it go,
And now the air is shattered by the force of Casey's blow.

Oh, somewhere in this favored land the sun is shining bright;
The band is playing somewhere, and somewhere hearts are light,
And somewhere men are laughing, and somewhere children shout;
But there is no joy in Mudville—mighty Casey has struck out.

SPEECH EXERCISES

By sixth grade, students should be able to work with accompaniments, speech rounds, and quodlibets with confidence. When working with variations on speech exercises, make sure that the students know the verse well enough that they can hold their own and not be overly distracted by the other elements. Varying the groups responsible for the different accompaniments helps students to hear the poem as a whole.

Both "Trouble" and "Fat Cats" work well as rounds and/or with accompaniments. I have provided several accompaniments but encourage you and your students to create your own. Both of these poems work well as assembly presentations.

Trouble
David Keppel

Better never trouble Trouble
Until Trouble troubles you;
For you only make your trouble
Double-trouble when you do;
And the trouble—like a bubble—
That you're troubling about,
May be nothing but a cipher
With its rim rubbed out.

Possible Accompaniments:

1. I'm in so much trouble
   Trouble caused by you;
   I'm in so much trouble
   What am I to do?

2. What did I do to get in such trouble?
   What did I do to get in this mess?
   What did I do to get in such trouble?
   How can I ever get out of this mess?

3. Trouble trouble, double trouble
   Double trouble has found me.
   Trouble trouble, double trouble
   How can I ever get free?

4. You're in trouble, uh-huh,
   Double trouble, uh-huh
   You're in trouble, uh-huh
   Double trouble, uh-huh

Fat Cats, Red Hats

If fat cats all wore hats,
Red hats to wear in bed;
They would never catch any rats
'Cause rats hate cats in red.

Possible Accompaniments:

1. Cats say: Oh how I love my red hat
   Rats say: I hate red! I hate red!

2. Look at all those fat cats
   Wearing bright red hats
   They won't catch a single rat
   While lying down in bed.

Many of the following poems can be done as rounds, and I encourage you and your students to compose humorous accompaniments.

The Blazer Braid

I brought the blazer braid I bought
To bind the blazer blue.
The braid I bought was much too bright
To bind the blazer blue.

Need a Needle?

I need not your needles
They're needless to me
For the needing of needles
Is needless, you see.
But did my neat trousers
But need to be kneed
Then I should have need
Of your needles indeed.

Roasting Roaches

Freddy is ready to roast red roaches,
For breakfast or dinner or lunch'
Are you ready for Freddy's fresh roasted red roaches?
I'm sure you will like how they crunch.

Bleeding Beetles

One black beetle bled black blood,
While another black beetle bled blue.
Prick the first beetle with a very sharp needle
To make sure that he doesn't bleed blue.
Prick the first beetle with a very sharp needle
To make sure that he doesn't bleed blue.

But if that beetle bleeds black blood
Instead of bleeding blue,
Prick the second beetle with a very sharp needle
And I'm sure he will bleed blue.
Prick the second beetle with a very sharp needle
And I'm sure he will bleed blue.

The Twister of Twists

A twister of twists once twisted a twist,
And the twist that he twisted was a three-twisted twist.
Now in twisting the twist, if a twist should untwist,
The twist that untwisted would untwist the twist.

Bitter Biting Bitterns

A bitter biting bittern
Bit a better brother bittern,
And the bitter better bittern
Bit the bitter biter back.
And the bitter bittern, bitten,
By the better bitten bittern,
Said: "I'm a bitter biter bit, alack!"

Quodlibets

A musical quodlibet is a composition that combines different melodies. For instance, "Row, Row, Row Your Boat" can be combined with "Frère Jacques" and/or with "Three Blind Mice" because these three tunes have a similar rhythmic structure and melodies that blend harmoniously.

A speech quodlibet combines different poems either concurrently or as a round. For instance "Hugh the Hewer" can be combined with "A Hop to Tahiti" to create a rich texture. These poems can also be done as rounds, with one group starting with one poem and the other group with the other poem. The second time they recite them, they can switch poems. For an extra challenge, you can have students recite the first line of one poem, the second line of the other poem, the third line of the first poem, etc. The second time they recite them they recite the first line of the second poem, the second line of the first poem, the third line of the second poem, etc.

The following poems can be recited with accompaniments, as rounds, and as quodlibets.

Hugh the Hewer

In Huron a hewer, Hugh Hughes,
Hewed yews of unusual hues.
Hugh Hughes used blue yews
To build sheds for his ewes;
So his ewes a blue-hued ewe-shed use.

A Hop to Tahiti

Heather was hoping to hop to Tahiti
To hack a hibiscus to hang on her hat.
Now Heather has hundreds of hats on her hat rack,
So how can a hop to Tahiti help that?

Pirate Booty

Blackbeard brought back black bric-a-brac.
Bluebeard brought back blue bric-a-brac.
Black bric-a-brac or blue—
Which bric-a-brac suits you?

Mutter Shutter

Once I heard a mother utter:
"Daughter, go and shut the shutter!"
"Shutter's shut!" the daughter muttered,
"I can't shut it any shutter!"

Dusting the Bust

A maid with a duster made a furious bluster
Dusting a bust in a hall.
The bust it was dusted; the bust it was busted
The bust it was dust, that is all.

TONGUE TWISTERS

Tongue twisters can be recited in their own right or as warm-ups for recitations. Because tongue twisters are so short and catchy, students can memorize them easily and say them quickly and correctly after a few attempts. When working with tongue twisters, check that your students are enunciating clearly, especially once they begin to recite rapidly.

I usually worked with group of three or four tongue twisters for about a week at a time, adding variations as the students became more adept. It is important to move on to new tongue twisters before the ones you have been working on get stale. Many of the tongue twisters from the other grades are appropriate for sixth grade, so if you want additional options, refer to those chapters.

Tongue Twister Variations

The simplest way to bring variety into your work with tongue twisters is to change the tempo, but there are other techniques that also can make the tongue twister more interesting and challenging. These variations should be used sparingly, because students don't like to belabor them.

1. Once they have learned the tongue twister, have the students guess how many times the primary sound occurs. Have them check their guess.

2. In a frivolous vein, have students exaggerate the primary sound. For instance:
   The **B**leak **B**reeze **B**lights the **B**right **B**room **B**lossom.

They can also recite the tongue twister using different accents or taking on a persona.

3. Challenge your students to recite the tongue twister leaving out the primary sound. For instance:
   The _leak _reeze _lights the _right _room _lossom.

The next two variations work well when each student says the next word in the tongue twister. The challenge is not to let the tongue twister become choppy or disjointed. At first, you can go down the rows, so students can anticipate who speaks next. Eventually, you can point to the students randomly so that they all have to remain alert.

4. Turn the tongue twister into a progressive exercise by adding a new word each time. For instance

    The
    The bleak
    The bleak breeze
    The bleak breeze blights

The bleak breeze blights the
The bleak breeze blights the bright
The bleak breeze blights the bright broom
The bleak breeze blights the bright broom blossom.

5. Turn the tongue twister into a progressive exercise by adding a new word backwards. For instance:

blossom
broom blossom
bright broom blossom
the bright broom blossom
blights the bright broom blossom
breeze blights the bright broom blossom
bleak breeze blights the bright broom blossom
The bleak breeze blights the bright broom blossom.

6. For a final challenge, have students try to recite the tongue twister in reverse order.

The bleak breeze blights the bright broom blossom.
Blossom broom bright the blights breeze bleak the

After saying the tongue twister in reverse order several times, some students will be able to say it fluently without much effort.

A Selection of Tongue Twisters[4]

Three blue beads in a blue bladder rattle.
Blue beads; bladder; blue rattle

Beautiful, babbling brooks bubble between blossoming banks.

I bought the blazer braid I bought to bind the blazer blue
The braid I bought was not too bright to bind the blazer blue.

Plain bun, plum bun, bun without plum.

Conrad came careering round the corner
Completing his crazy career by crashing into the crypt.

How can a clam cram in a clean cream can?

---

[4] Additional tongue twisters can be found at the ends of the chapters for 5th, 7th, and 8th Grades.

Crows graze in droves
on grass which grows
on graves in groves.

Top chopstick shops stock top chopsticks
while cheap chop-suey shops stock cheap soup chips.

Mrs. Chip is very old, and when she settles down to stitch—
Unless she uses spectacles—she cannot see which stitch is which.

Dashing dangerously down the dale,
Dainty Dinah dashed dizzily past Dorothy.

Double bubble gum bubbles double.

For French shrimp try a French shrimp shop;
For fresh fish try Fred's fish fry.

Fifteen frightened fluffy fowls fly foolishly through the farmyard.

A fine field of wheat
A field of fine wheat

George Gabs grabs crabs,
Crabs George Gabs grabs.
If George Gabs grabs crabs
Where are the crabs George grabs?

"Goodbye, Gerty," gushed Gussie.
"Goodbye, Gussie," gushed Gerty.

Hard-hearted Harold hit Henry hard
with a hickory-handled iron hammer.
Henry howled horribly and hurriedly hobbled home.

A hunter went a-hunting, a-hunting for a hare,
But where he thought the hare would be, he found a hairy bear.

Red leather, yellow leather. Red leather, yellow leather. Red leather, yellow leather.

A lump of red leather, a red leather lump;
A lump of red leather from Old Yeller's rump.

Many an anemone sees an enemy anemone.

On mules we find two legs behind
and two we find before.
We stand behind before we find
what those behind be for.

Your imbecilic mimicking is sickening.

Mother's mellow miracle mustard makes most moldy meat much more munchable.

Can you imagine an imaginary menagerie manager
Imagining managing an imaginary menagerie?

Mortals may not match my magic muttered the magician menacingly.

I need not your needles, they're needless to me,
For the needing of needles is needless, you see;
But did my neat trousers but need to be kneed,
Then I should have need of your needles indeed.

The bold toad told the cold mole how he sold his moldy coal.

Peggy Babcock.
Peggy Babcock.
Peggy Babcock.
Peggy Babcock.
Peggy Babcock.

Please Paul, pause for applause.
Pause for applause, Paul.

Is there a pleasant peasant present?

Put the cut pumpkin in a pipkin.

If practice makes perfect and perfect needs practice,
I'm perfectly practiced and practically perfect.

A pessimistic pest exists amidst us.

Quick — Quack — Quock;
Quack — Quock — Quick;
Quock — Quick — Quack.

Richard gave Robin a rap in the ribs for roasting his rabbit so rare.

Recitation in Sixth Grade

Don't run along the wrong lane.

Stanley sat sadly solitary
sipping sodas sloppily
near the Mississippi.

Swiftly slide the slippery snakes,
See them slither by,
Softly over stock and stone,
Slipping on the sly.

Six sick hicks nick six slick bricks with picks and sticks.

I shot the city sheriff. I shot the city sheriff. I shot the city sheriff.

Susan shineth shoes and socks
Socks and shoes shines Susan.
She ceaseth shining shoes and socks,
For socks and shoes shock Susan.

Suddenly swerving, seven small swans
Swam silently southward,
When they saw six swift sailboats
Sailing sedately seaward.

The old school scold sold the school coal scuttle.
If the old school scold sold the school coal scuttle,
The school should scold and scuttle the old school scold.

Sheila's Shetland pony shied,
Shooting Sheila on the shore.
Shaking Sheila, stupefied,
Struggled homeward stiff and sore.

Sheep shouldn't sleep in a shack;
Sheep should sleep in a shed.

Shut up the shutters and sit in the shop!

She sells seashells on the seashore.
The shells she sells are seashells, I'm sure.

I'm a sheet slitter. I slit sheets.
I'm the sleekest sheet slitter that ever slit sheets.

There's a slit in the sheet; the sheet is slit;
Upon the slitted sheet I sit.

I sit and slit and slit and sit; upon the slitted sheet I sit.

Please sell me some short silk socks and some shimmering satin sashes.

Sooty Sukey shook some soot
From Sister Susi's sooty Shoes.

One smart fellow, he felt smart.
Two smart fellows, they felt smart.
Three smart fellows, they all felt smart.

The miller shifts six sacks with care.
And first sifts three, the first three there.
Then when the fourth and fifth are past,
He sifts the sixth sack last.

The seething sea ceaseth seething.

Some seventy-six sad seasick seamen soon set sail
seeking soothing, salty South Sea sunshine.

If she stops at the shop where I stop
And shops at the shop where I shop,
Then I shan't stop to shop at the shop
Where she stops to shop.

Seventy shuddering sailors standing silent
As short, sharp, shattering shocks shake their splendid ship.

Thin-skinned Slim, thinking Theda's statements scurrilous, scolded scathingly.

Rick's spitz Fritz threw snits and fits.

Till Tom taught tact to Tim, Tim talked trash to tots.

Tim's twin sisters sing tongue twisters.

Ted threw Fred three free throws;
Fred threw Ted three free throws.

Three free thugs set three thugs free.

Tom bought some fine prime pink popcorn from the prime pink popcorn shop.

Ten tiny toddling tots trying to train their tongues to trill.

Theophilus Thistledown, the successful thistle-sifter,
In sifting a sieve of unsifted thistles,
Thrust three thousand thistles through the thick of his thumb.

If Theophilus Thistledown, the successful thistle-sifter,
Thrust three thousand thistles through the thick of his thumb,
See that thou, in sifting thistles,
Stick not the thistles through the thick of thy thumb.

Will you, William?
William. Will you?
Will you, William?
William. Will you?

Can't you, William?
William can't you?
Won't you, William?
William. Won't you?

Can't you, William,
Won't you, William,
Don't you, William, don't you.

Why do you cry, Willy?
Why do you cry?
Why, Willy?
Why, Willy?
Why? Willy? Why?

Willie's really weary.
Willie's really weary.
Willie's really weary.
Really weary Willie.

Wiles and snares
And snares and wiles
Of a snary, wiley world.

Recitation in Seventh Grade

Most seventh graders are at some stage of passing through puberty. As a result, they feel self-conscious and are very concerned about how others see them, causing them to withdraw inwardly or to show off outwardly. Seventh graders are looking for examples and exemplars of remarkable people who have been tested by life. That is why the biographies of people like Joan of Arc, Martin Luther, or Galileo appeal to them so much. Seventh graders have lost the natural confidence of ten- or eleven-year-olds; now they doubt themselves, but they also seek opportunities to prove themselves equal to life's challenges.

The recitation curriculum for seventh grade includes selections from the history curriculum, lyric and narrative poems, speech exercises, and tongue twisters. The lyric poems express the variety and nuances of human experiences, while narrative poems and the recitations from history help students find a relationship to the questions and challenges faced by strong individuals.

In seventh grade, Morning Exercises continue to play an important role in getting the students ready for Main Lesson. These exercises should be divided into sections that allow the class to focus on speech, music, concentration exercises, and movement activities. In general, Morning Exercise routines benefit from being coordinated with the Main Lesson blocks, but some of the selections or activities don't warrant three or four weeks, so they can be replaced as necessary.

Recitations should no longer be done chorally except on rare occasions. Instead, students should be able to recite selections on their own, and I recommend that at the end of the block, students have an opportunity to demonstrate their mastery. Those who are most confident should go first, allowing those who feel shakier to hear the recitation many times before their turn.

Speech exercises should strive for a new level of complexity without sacrificing clarity or nuance. The techniques that were introduced in younger grades—accompaniments, rounds, and quodlibets—can now be used in interesting combinations. At this age, students are eager to suggest variations, and I encourage you to try them. Many seventh graders have a quirky sense of humor, so in addition to humorous speech exercises, consider including limericks in your speech work. If you decide to work on limericks, I suggest that you focus on immediate recall until students can recite a limerick that they have heard only once. Because limericks are so formulaic, they are easy to compose, so students can be challenged to compose their own limericks, which can then be recited by the class.

Seventh graders enjoy tongue twisters because they provide an opportunity to improve enunciation and to develop greater agility. Because seventh graders master tongue twisters so quickly, they should be recited with variations and not be worked on too long so that they don't become stale. Detailed instructions about different ways to work with tongue twisters may be found on pages 38–41, 69–75, 105–109, and 152–154.

Before beginning to work on a recitation, you should introduce it. Recitations about curricular subjects need no introduction, because the Main Lesson presentation will have provided the context. For all other selections, introductions should include the title and the author of the work, and, if you wish, something about the author's life and the work's background and context.

Next you should provide a brief summary of the work and speak about the important themes, people, or events. If the form and style of the work are important, they should be mentioned, and if any literary devices are used, they should be highlighted.

Introductions to works with particularly meaningful themes, characters, or events should include your comments. I encourage you to express your opinion freely because your students will learn a great deal, not only about the recitation, but about you. Introductions to important works can also include a class discussion that explores the work's importance and relevance. These discussions strengthen the class community as the students get to know each other better, and they deepen our bond with our students as we express what we think and believe.

What has been described all occurs *before* students hear the work for the first time. This approach may seem counter-intuitive because we typically discuss and analyze a work *after* we have heard it. But this approach appeals to the students' feelings, especially to their curiosity and interest. And when they hear the work for the first time, students will connect with the work more completely, understand more it deeply, and appreciate it more fully.

If you wish to learn more about this novel approach, please refer to Discussion 6 of *Discussions with Teachers*, where Rudolf Steiner demonstrated how a teacher might introduce a fable or a poem. If you are new to this method, I encourage you to try it. Although you may feel a bit awkward at first, I believe that you will quickly experience how well it works.

Morning Exercises help students put aside their everyday lives and to begin to focus on the demands of the school day. They should not exceed 20–25 minutes per day, however, because when they are too long, students can become less attentive and responsive, and they may have difficulty concentrating on their work. Morning Exercises are important, but we need to remember that they are only a preparation for—not a major component of—the Main Lesson.

YEARLY VERSES

Verses that are recited throughout the year have a special place in the speech curriculum. The daily repetition of these verses imprints them in the students' hearts and affirms life-long ideals. Because a verse that is recited daily can end up being done without much thought, I recommend occasionally to bring it to consciousness by discussing the meaning and importance of the theme or a special phrase, and/or using it as a writing prompt.

A typical seventh-grade Main Lesson might begin with announcements, class housekeeping, and/or a check-in. I think that these should all precede the recitation of the Morning Verse so that the verse can mark the formal beginning of the Main Lesson. If possible, all the upper grades in your school should use the same version of the verse because this builds a sense of community among the classes. I have therefore not included versions of the Morning Verse because each school needs to find the one seems best.

My students and I recited the following verses all year long: the Morning Verse at the beginning of Main Lesson; "There Lives in Me an Image" at the end of the Morning Exercises; "May Wisdom Shine through Me" at the end of the Main Lesson; and "At the Ringing of the Bells" at the end of the day.

Angelus Silesius was the name that Johann Scheffler (1624–1677) adopted when he became a Catholic priest and composed many religious poems that expressed his mystical beliefs. My classes recited "There Lives in Me an Image" for all eight years of our journey because I hoped that it might become a motto for their lives.

There Lives in Me an Image
Angelus Silesius

There lives in me an image,
Of all that I should be;
Until I have become it,
My heart is never free.

We also recited "May Wisdom Shine through Me" at the end of Main Lesson throughout the grades. Like "There Lives in Me an Image," it expresses ideals that I wanted to reinforce through daily repetition over many years.

May Wisdom Shine through Me
Rudolf Steiner

May wisdom shine through me,
May love glow within me,
May strength permeate me,
That in me may arise
A helper of humankind,
A server of holy things,
Selfless and true.

At the end of the day we recited "At the Ringing of the Bells," which serves as a meaningful bookend to the Morning Verse.

At the Ringing of the Bells
Rudolf Steiner

To wonder at beauty,
Stand guard over truth,
Look up to the noble,
Decide for the good—
Leads us on our journey
To goals for our life:
To right in our doing;
To peace in our feeling;
To light in our thought.
And teaches us trust
In the guidance of God;
In all that there is—
In the world-wide All,
In the soul's deep soil.

RECITATIONS FROM THE CURRICULUM

The seventh-grade history curriculum includes the European Age of Exploration, the Renaissance, the Reformation, and the Age of Scientific Discovery. Recitations about these themes enrich the students' experience of the events and people they study.

John Masefield (1878–1967) was an English writer who served as the British Poet Laureate for almost forty years. In his youth, he spent several years at sea, and his voyages made a strong impression on him. While at sea, he loved to listen to sailors' stories, which inspired him become a storyteller.

In your introduction, you might speak about the scenes and experiences that can cause a sailor to yearn to return to the sea. You might also draw the students' attention to John Masefield's choice of words that convey clear images, and to the cadences of his lines that create a sense of movement.

Sea Fever
John Masefield

I must down to the seas again, to the lonely sea and the sky,
And all I ask is a tall ship and a star to steer her by;
And the wheel's kick and the wind's song and the white sail's shaking,
And a grey mist on the sea's face, and a grey dawn breaking.

I must down to the seas again, for the call of the running tide
Is a wild call and a clear call that may not be denied;
And all I ask is a windy day with the white clouds flying,
And the flung spray and the blown spume, and the sea-gulls crying.

I must down to the seas again, to the vagrant gypsy life,
To the gull's way and the whale's way where the wind's like a whetted knife;
And all I ask is a merry yarn from a laughing fellow-rover,
And quiet sleep and a sweet dream when the long trick's over.

Allan Cunningham (1784–1842) was a Scottish poet and author who enjoyed writing Scottish ballads in their traditional style. When introducing this poem, you might tell the students that it was composed as lyrics to a song. As the students learn the poem, encourage them to emphasize the rhythm, which creates a sense of movement and momentum.

A Wet Sheet and a Flowing Sea
Allan Cunningham

A wet sheet and a flowing sea,
   A wind that follows fast
And fills the white and rustling sail
   And bends the gallant mast;
And bends the gallant mast, my boys,
   While like the eagle free
Away the good ship flies, and leaves
   Old England on the lee.

O for a soft and gentle wind!
   I heard a fair one cry;
But give to me the snoring breeze
   And white waves heaving high;
And white waves heaving high, my lads,
   The good ship tight and free—
The world of waters is our home,
   And merry men are we.

There's tempest in yon horned moon,
   And lightning in yon cloud;
But hark the music, mariners!
   The wind is piping loud;
The wind is piping loud, my boys,
   The lightning flashes free—
While the hollow oak our palace is,
   Our heritage the sea.

European explorers have become controversial historical figures. You will have to determine whether and how to work with the themes and paradoxes of their lives and deeds, and to help the students recognize that, in their time, people had very different values from ours. If you decide to share Columbus's biography, you might wish to read or have the students learn to recite this famous poem by Joaquin Miller (1837–1913), who was an explorer and frontiersman. This poem can be recited with different groups or individuals speaking the various parts.

Columbus
Joaquin Miller

Behind him lay the gray Azores,
Behind the Gates of Hercules;
Before him not the ghost of shores,
Before him only shoreless seas.
The good mate said: "Now we must pray,
For lo! the very stars are gone.
Brave Admiral, speak, what shall I say?
"Why, say, 'Sail on! sail on! and on!' "

"My men grow mutinous day by day;
My men grow ghastly wan and weak."
The stout mate thought of home; a spray
Of salt wave washed his swarthy cheek.
"What shall I say, brave Admiral, say,
If we sight naught but seas at dawn?"
"Why, you shall say at break of day,
'Sail on! sail on! and on!' "

They sailed and sailed, as winds might blow,
Until at last the blanched mate said:
"Why, now not even God would know
Should I and all my men fall dead.
These very winds forget their way,
For God from these dead seas is gone.
Now speak, brave Admiral, speak and say"—
He said, "Sail on! sail on! and on!"

They sailed. They sailed. Then spake the mate:
"This mad sea shows his teeth tonight.
He curls his lip, he lies in wait,
With lifted teeth, as if to bite!
Brave Admiral, say but one good word:
What shall we do when hope is gone?"
The words leapt like a leaping sword:
"Sail on! sail on! sail on! and on!"

Then pale and worn, he kept his deck,
And peered through darkness. Ah, that night
Of all dark nights! And then a speck —
A light! a light! at last a light!
It grew, a starlit flag unfurled!
It grew to be Time's burst of dawn.
He gained a world; he gave that world
Its grandest lesson: "On! sail on!"

Lizette Woodworth Reese (1856–1935) was a long-time teacher, who was named Poet Laureate of Maryland. When you introduce this poem, you might remind the students of the important places in the life of Joan of Arc. Draw their attention to the images the poet chose to convey a melancholic mood. Point out the last lines of the stanzas and discuss how the poem's message is reinforced by this repetition.

The Good Joan
Lizette Woodworth Reese

Along the thousand roads of France,
Now there, now here, swift as a glance,
A cloud, a mist blown down the sky,
Good Joan of Arc goes riding by.

In Domremy at candlelight,
The orchards blowing rose and white
About the shadowy houses lie;
And Joan of Arc goes riding by.

On Avignon there falls a hush,
Brief as the singing of a thrush
Across old gardens April-high;
And Joan of Arc goes riding by.

The women bring the apples in,
Round Arles when the long gusts begin,
Then sit them down to sob and cry;
And Joan of Arc goes riding by.

Dim fall the hoofs down old Calais;
In Tours a flash of silver-gray,
Like flaw of rain in a clear sky;
And Joan of Arc goes riding by.

Who saith that ancient France shall fail,
A rotting leaf driv'n down the gale?
Then her sons know not how to die;
Then good God dwells no more on high!
Tours, Arles, and Domremy reply!
For Joan of Arc goes riding by.

The three next recitations capture the essence of the individuals who are quoted. If possible, include these passages in the presentation about the person's life, and then have the students learn and recite them. I suggest having every student learn at least one of these passages and reciting it alone. All the other students who have learned the passage will follow along, inwardly participating in the recitation.

The Speech at the Diet of Worms (excerpt)
Martin Luther

Unless I am convicted by Scripture or by plain reason—for I trust neither in popes nor in councils, since they have often erred and contradicted themselves—unless I am thus convicted, I am bound by the text of the Bible and my conscience is captive to the word of God. I neither can nor will recant anything, for to act against conscience it is neither right nor safe. Here I stand; I can do no other. God help me. Amen.

Quote
Nicholas Copernicus

To look up at the sky, and behold the wondrous works of God, must make a man bow his head and heart in silence. I have thought and studied and worked for years, and I know so little. All I can do is to adore when I behold this unfailing regularity, this miraculous balance and perfect adaptation. The majesty of it all humbles me to the dust.

Quote
Isaac Newton

I do not know what I may appear to the world, but to myself I seem to have been only like a boy playing on the seashore, and diverting myself in now and then finding a smoother pebble or a prettier shell than ordinary, whilst the great ocean of truth lay all undiscovered before me.

The study of Health and Human Physiology completes the arc of the Nature Study curriculum, which begins with the human being in relationship to the animal world in the fourth grade, then considers the plant world, the minerals, and heavenly bodies in fifth and sixth grade before returning to the human being in seventh grade. This speech from *Antigone* (441 BCE) expresses the ancient Greek view of the specialness of the human being. In your introduction, you might discuss which human qualities distinguish us from the animals.

Antigone (excerpt)
Sophocles

Numberless are the world's wonders, but none
More wonderful than man; the storm gray sea
Yields to his prows, the huge crests bear him high;
Earth, holy and inexhaustible, is graven
With shining furrows where his plows have gone
Year after year, the timeless labor of stallions.

The light-boned birds and beasts that cling to cover,
The lithe fish lighting their reaches of dim water,
All are taken, tamed in the net of his mind;
The lion on the hill, the wild horse windy-maned,
Resign to him; and his blunt yoke has broken
The sultry shoulders of the mountain bull.

Words also, and thought as rapid as air,
He fashions to his good use; statecraft is his
And his the skill that deflects the arrows of snow,
The spears of winter rain: from every wind
He has made himself secure—from all but one:
In the late wind of death he cannot stand.

William Wordsworth (1770–1850) was one of the foremost English Romantic poets. His language and images appeal to seventh graders because of their lyricism. The entire ode from which this excerpt is taken is worth reviewing, because it portrays how we change in the course of our lives. I have used this excerpt during the Health and Human Physiology block to stimulate a discussion about where were we before we were born, and what happens to us after we die.

Ode: Intimations of Immortality
William Wordsworth

Our birth is but a sleep and a forgetting:
The Soul that rises with us, our life's Star,
      Hath had elsewhere its setting,
      And cometh from afar:
      Not in entire forgetfulness,
      And not in utter nakedness,

But trailing clouds of glory do we come
        From God, who is our home:
Heaven lies about us in our infancy!
Shades of the prison-house begin to close
        Upon the growing Boy,
But he beholds the light, and whence it flows,
        He sees it in his joy;
The Youth, who daily farther from the east
        Must travel, still is Nature's Priest,
        And by the vision splendid
        Is on his way attended;
At length the Man perceives it die away,
And fade into the light of common day.

LYRICAL POEMS

Robert Frost (1874–1963) was one of the best-known American poets of his time. Like many of his poems, "The Road Not Taken" is set in New England. In this poem, Robert Frost presents a seemingly simple situation that poses a meaningful question: Which path should I take on the road of life?

In your introduction, you might set the scene that the traveler confronts: diverging roads that differ slightly in terms of their use. You might consider the metaphor of the road of life and pose the question the traveler faces. Before revealing his choice and the difference that it made, you might ask the students which road they would choose if they were the traveler. You might also ask them to consider what kinds of life choices can make "all the difference." This poem lends itself to use as a writing prompt asking the students to consider the consequences of a choice they have made.

The Road Not Taken
Robert Frost

Two roads diverged in a yellow wood,
And sorry I could not travel both
And be one traveler, long I stood
And looked down one as far as I could
To where it bent in the undergrowth;

Then took the other, as just as fair,
And having perhaps the better claim
Because it was grassy and wanted wear;
Though as for that, the passing there
Had worn them really about the same,

And both that morning equally lay
In leaves no step had trodden black.
Oh, I kept the first for another day!
Yet knowing how way leads on to way,
I doubted if I should ever come back.

I shall be telling this with a sigh
Somewhere ages and ages hence:
Two roads diverged in a wood, and I
I took the one less traveled by,
And that has made all the difference.

William Butler Yeats (1865–1939) was one of the foremost poets of the early 20th century. In your introduction to this poem, you might have a conversation with the students about the urge to "get away from it all" that many of us feel at some point in our lives. Students might also be introduced to the images in each stanza and how they develop and reinforce the poet's expression of his yearning for peace. This poem might be used as a writing prompt about a special place where we feel more fully at home and at peace.

Lake Isle of Innisfree
William Butler Yeats

I will arise and go now, and go to Innisfree,
And a small cabin build there, of clay and wattles made;
Nine bean-rows will I have there, a hive for the honey-bee,
And live alone in the bee-loud glade.

And I shall have some peace there, for peace comes dropping slow,
Dropping from the veils of the morning to where the cricket sings;
There midnight's all a glimmer, and noon a purple glow,
And evening full of the linnet's wings.

I will arise and go now, for always night and day
I hear lake water lapping with low sounds by the shore;
While I stand on the roadway, or on the pavements grey,
I hear it in the deep heart's core.

Anne Brontë (1820–1849) was the youngest of the Brontë sisters. Anne wrote two novels, but they did not achieve the fame of *Wuthering Heights* by Emily Brontë or *Jane Eyre* by Charlotte Brontë. "Lines Composed in a Wood on a Windy Day" appeals to seventh graders because of its earnest voice and vivid images. Your introduction might consider the physical effects of the wind and the feelings that the wind arouses.

Lines Composed in a Wood on a Windy Day
Anne Brontë

My soul is awakened, my spirit is soaring
    And carried aloft on the winds of the breeze;
For above and around me the wild wind is roaring,
    Arousing to rapture the earth and the seas.
The long withered grass in the sunshine is glancing,
    The bare trees are tossing their branches on high;
The dead leaves beneath them are merrily dancing,
    The white clouds are scudding across the blue sky.
I wish I could see how the ocean is lashing
    The foam of its billows to whirlwinds of spray;
I wish I could see how its proud waves are dashing,
    And hear the wild roar of their thunder to-day!

As adolescents begin to exercise their powers of judgment, they view themselves, other people, and the world differently. The introduction to this poem might include a conversation about what makes a life "well-lived." You might also ask the students to contrast a ship that sails with one that remains at port or in dry dock.

The Ship That Sails
attributed to Page Belnap

I'd rather be the ship that sails
—And rides the billows wild and free;
Than to be the ship that always fails
—To leave its port and go to sea.

I'd rather feel the sting of strife,
—Where gales are born and tempests roar;
Than to settle down to useless life
—And rot in dry dock on the shore.

I'd rather fight some mighty wave
—With honor in supreme command;
And fill at last a well-earned grave,
—Than die in ease upon the sand.

I'd rather drive where sea storms blow,
—And be the ship that always failed.
To make the ports where it would go,
—Than be the ship that never sailed.

Students will probably have recited poems by Emily Dickinson (1830–1886) in earlier grades. If they haven't heard her biography, they will enjoy hearing about the reclusive "Belle of Amherst." Emily Dickinson was a prolific poet and included poems in her letters to friends, but only a small fraction of her poems were published during her lifetime. After her death, her family discovered forty hand-bound volumes containing approximately 1,800 poems. "If I Can Stop One Heart from Breaking" is a quintessential Emily Dickinson poem—clear, direct, and expressing a noble sentiment.

If I Can Stop One Heart From Breaking
Emily Dickinson

If I can stop one heart from breaking,
I shall not live in vain;
If I can ease one life the aching,
Or cool one pain,
Or help one fainting robin
Unto his nest again,
I shall not live in vain.

The Romantic poet, John Keats (1795–1821), was a contemporary of Lord Byron and Percy Bysshe Shelley. He died at the age of 25, having published his first works four years earlier. "To Autumn," the last of his six odes, is considered one of the most perfect short poems in the English language. In your introduction you might consider John Keats's choice of words and images that express the theme of each of the stanzas.

To Autumn
John Keats

Season of mists and mellow fruitfulness,
    Close bosom-friend of the maturing sun;
Conspiring with him how to load and bless
    With fruit the vines that round the thatch-eves run;
To bend with apples the moss'd cottage-trees,
    And fill all fruit with ripeness to the core;
    To swell the gourd, and plump the hazel shells
    With a sweet kernel; to set budding more,
And still more, later flowers for the bees,
Until they think warm days will never cease,
    For summer has o'er-brimm'd their clammy cells.

Who hath not seen thee oft amid thy store?
    Sometimes whoever seeks abroad may find
Thee sitting careless on a granary floor,
    Thy hair soft-lifted by the winnowing wind;
Or on a half-reap'd furrow sound asleep,
    Drows'd with the fume of poppies, while thy hook
    Spares the next swath and all its twined flowers:
And sometimes like a gleaner thou dost keep
    Steady thy laden head across a brook;
    Or by a cyder-press, with patient look,
    Thou watchest the last oozings hours by hours.

Where are the songs of spring? Ay, Where are they?
    Think not of them, thou hast thy music too,—
While barred clouds bloom the soft-dying day,
    And touch the stubble-plains with rosy hue;
Then in a wailful choir the small gnats mourn
    Among the river sallows, borne aloft
    Or sinking as the light wind lives or dies;
And full-grown lambs loud bleat from hilly bourn;
    Hedge-crickets sing; and now with treble soft
    The red-breast whistles from a garden-croft;
    And gathering swallows twitter in the skies.

Edgar Allan Poe (1809–1849) is best known for his tales of mystery and the macabre, some of which can be read by the students as part of their study of literature. In your introduction, you might tell the students a bit about Poe's short, dramatic life. You might also explore how the poet's use of repetition reinforces the poem's message.

Annabel Lee
Edgar Allan Poe

It was many and many a year ago,
    In a kingdom by the sea,
That a maiden there lived whom you may know
    By the name of Annabel Lee;
And this maiden she lived with no other thought
    Than to love and be loved by me.

I was a child and *she* was a child,
    In this kingdom by the sea,
But we loved with a love that was more than love—
    I and my Annabel Lee—
With a love that the wingèd seraphs of Heaven
    Coveted her and me.

And this was the reason that, long ago,
   In this kingdom by the sea,
A wind blew out of a cloud, chilling
   My beautiful Annabel Lee;
So that her highborn kinsmen came
   And bore her away from me,
To shut her up in a sepulchre
   In this kingdom by the sea.

The angels, not half so happy in Heaven,
   Went envying her and me—
Yes!—that was the reason (as all men know,
   In this kingdom by the sea)
That the wind came out of the cloud by night,
   Chilling and killing my Annabel Lee.

But our love it was stronger by far than the love
   Of those who were older than we—
   Of many far wiser than we—
And neither the angels in Heaven above
   Nor the demons down under the sea
Can ever dissever my soul from the soul
   Of the beautiful Annabel Lee;

For the moon never beams, without bringing me dreams
   Of the beautiful Annabel Lee;
And the stars never rise, but I feel the bright eyes
   Of the beautiful Annabel Lee;
And so, all the night-tide, I lie down by the side
   Of my darling—my darling—my life and my bride,
   In her sepulchre there by the sea—
   In her tomb by the sounding sea.

Maya Angelou (1928–2014) was a prolific American writer whose autobiography *I Know Why the Caged Bird Sings*, brought her international acclaim. Maya Angelou worked in the civil rights movement with Dr. Martin Luther King Jr. and Malcolm X, and her work reflects her search for social justice.

"Caged Bird" could be learned in seventh grade as a powerful contrast between freedom and enslavement or it could be learned in the eighth grade as part of the study of the African-American experience. Your introduction might provide a biographical sketch of Maya Angelou's life and a consideration of the contrast between the life of a free bird and a caged bird. This poem can also be used as a writing prompt that asks the students to consider an imprisoning aspect of their life.

Caged Bird
Maya Angelou

A free bird leaps
on the back of the wind
and floats downstream
till the current ends
and dips his wing
in the orange sun rays
and dares to claim the sky.

But a bird that stalks
down his narrow cage
can seldom see through
his bars of rage
his wings are clipped and
his feet are tied
so he opens his throat to sing.

The caged bird sings
with a fearful trill
of things unknown
but longed for still
and his tune is heard
on the distant hill
for the caged bird
sings of freedom.

The free bird thinks of another breeze
and the trade winds soft through the sighing trees
and the fat worms waiting on a dawn bright lawn
and he names the sky his own.

But a caged bird stands on the grave of dreams
his shadow shouts on a nightmare scream
his wings are clipped and his feet are tied
so he opens his throat to sing.

The caged bird sings
with a fearful trill
of things unknown
but longed for still
and his tune is heard
on the distant hill
for the caged bird
sings of freedom.

Seventh graders have a keen appreciation for irony, and they love anecdotes and stories that have a surprise ending. I don't think this recitation needs an introduction, but it will benefit from a later discussion or a composition about destiny and whether we can escape it.

William Somerset Maugham (1874–1965) was a well-known English writer and playwright. His most famous work is *Of Human Bondage.*

The Appointment in Samarra
W. Somerset Maugham

There was a merchant in Baghdad who sent his servant to market to buy provisions and in a little while the servant came back, white and trembling, and said, Master, just now when I was in the marketplace I was jostled by a woman in the crowd and when I turned I saw it was Death that jostled me. She looked at me and made a threatening gesture, now, lend me your horse, and I will ride away from this city and avoid my fate. I will go to Samarra and there Death will not find me. The merchant lent him his horse, and the servant mounted it, and he dug his spurs in its flanks and as fast as the horse could gallop he went. Then the merchant went down to the marketplace and he saw me standing in the crowd and he came to me and said, Why did you make a threating gesture to my servant when you saw him this morning? That was not a threatening gesture, I said, it was only a start of surprise. I was astonished to see him in Baghdad, for I had an appointment with him tonight in Samarra.

NARRATIVE POEMS

In fifth and sixth grades, students started to learn longer poems, and now, in seventh grade, they will enjoy narrative poems that are dramatic, humorous, or ironic.

Thomas Campbell (1777–1844) was a Scottish poet whose poetry often dealt with patriotic themes. In this poem, he explores the different types of loyalty and allegiance. Your introduction might include a conversation that explores the theme of the conflict that can arise when following our heart clashes with our parents' wishes. This poem lends itself to dividing the various parts among groups or individuals.

Lord Ullin's Daughter
Thomas Campbell

A Chieftain, to the Highlands bound,
    Cries, "Boatman, do not tarry!
And I'll give thee a silver pound
    To row us o'er the ferry!"

"Now who be ye, would cross Lochgyle,
    This dark and stormy water?"
"O, I'm the chief of Ulva's isle,
    And this, Lord Ullin's daughter.

"And fast before her father's men
    Three days we've fled together,
For should he find us in the glen,
    My blood would stain the heather.

"His horsemen hard behind us ride;
    Should they our steps discover,
Then who will cheer my bonny bride
    When they have slain her lover?"

Out spoke the hardy Highland wight,
    "I'll go my chief, I'm ready:
It is not for your silver bright;
    But for your winsome lady:

"And by my word! the bonny bird
    In danger shall not tarry;
So, though the waves be raging white,
    I'll row you o'er the ferry."

By this the storm grew loud apace,
   The water wraith was shrieking;
And in the scowl of heaven each face
   Grew dark as they were speaking.

But still as wilder blew the wind
   And as the night grew drearer,
Adown the glen rode armed men,
   Their trampling sounded nearer.

"O haste thee, haste!" the lady cries,
   "Though tempests round us gather;
I'll meet the raging of the skies,
   But not an angry father."

The boat has left a stormy land,
   A stormy sea before her,
When O! too strong for human hand,
   The tempest gather'd o'er her.

And still they row'd amidst the roar
   Of waters fast prevailing:
Lord Ullin reach'd that fatal shore,
   His wrath was changed to wailing.

For, sore dismayed through storm and shade,
   His child he did discover:
One lovely hand she stretched for aid,
   And one was round her lover.

"Come back! come back!" he cried in grief
   "Across this stormy water:
And I'll forgive your Highland chief,
   My daughter! O my daughter!"

'Twas vain: the loud waves lashed the shore,
   Return or aid preventing;
The waters wild went o'er his child,
   And he was left lamenting.

George Gordon, Lord Byron, (1788–1824) was one of the most highly acclaimed English Romantic poets. He traveled widely in Europe and the Middle East and eventually settled abroad. "The Destruction of Sennacherib" is one of Byron's best-known poems. In your introduction, you might review the poem's vivid images and explore how these images convey strong feelings. You might also point out how the poem's rhythm engenders a sense of momentum. This poem lends itself to having different groups or individuals recite different stanzas or pairs of lines.

The Destruction of Sennacherib
George Gordon, Lord Byron

The Assyrian came down like the wolf on the fold,
And his cohorts were gleaming in purple and gold;
And the sheen of their spears was like stars on the sea,
When the blue wave rolls nightly on deep Galilee.

Like the leaves of the forest when Summer is green,
That host with their banners at sunset were seen:
Like the leaves of the forest when Autumn hath blown,
That host on the morrow lay withered and strown.

For the Angel of Death spread his wings on the blast,
And breathed in the face of the foe as he passed;
And the eyes of the sleepers waxed deadly and chill,
And their hearts but once heaved, and for ever grew still!

And there lay the steed with his nostril all wide,
But through it there rolled not the breath of his pride;
And the foam of his gasping lay white on the turf,
And cold as the spray of the rock-beating surf.

And there lay the rider distorted and pale,
With the dew on his brow, and the rust on his mail:
And the tents were all silent, the banners alone,
The lances unlifted, the trumpet unblown.

And the widows of Ashur are loud in their wail,
And the idols are broke in the temple of Baal;
And the might of the Gentile, unsmote by the sword,
Hath melted like snow in the glance of the Lord!

Alfred Noyes (1880–1958) was an English poet, novelist, and playwright. "The Highwayman" is one of his best-known works. Your introduction might include a conversation about the romance of outlaws, who live by their own creed. You might also draw the students' attention to the ways that Noyes uses vivid descriptions to engage the listener. Because this poem is so long, it may need to be divided into sections, with groups or individual students, reciting parts. If you don't wish to work on it as a recitation, you can have the students do a dramatic reading.

The Highwayman
Alfred Noyes

PART ONE

The wind was a torrent of darkness among the gusty trees.
The moon was a ghostly galleon tossed upon cloudy seas.
The road was a ribbon of moonlight over the purple moor,
And the highwayman came riding—
   Riding—riding—
The highwayman came riding, up to the old inn-door.

He'd a French cocked-hat on his forehead, a bunch of lace at his chin,
A coat of the claret velvet, and breeches of brown doe-skin.
They fitted with never a wrinkle. His boots were up to the thigh.
And he rode with a jeweled twinkle,
   His pistol butts a-twinkle,
His rapier hilt a-twinkle, under the jeweled sky.

Over the cobbles he clattered and clashed in the dark inn-yard.
He tapped with his whip on the shutters, but all was locked and barred.
He whistled a tune to the window, and who should be waiting there
But the landlord's black-eyed daughter,
   Bess, the landlord's daughter,
Plaiting a dark red love-knot into her long black hair.

And dark in the dark old inn-yard a stable-wicket creaked
Where Tim the ostler listened. His face was white and peaked.
His eyes were hollows of madness, his hair like moldy hay,
But he loved the landlord's daughter,
   The landlord's red-lipped daughter.
Dumb as a dog he listened, and he heard the robber say—

"One kiss, my bonny sweetheart, I'm after a prize to-night,
But I shall be back with the yellow gold before the morning light;
Yet, if they press me sharply, and harry me through the day,
Then look for me by moonlight,
   Watch for me by moonlight,
I'll come to thee by moonlight, though hell should bar the way."

He rose upright in the stirrups. He scarce could reach her hand,
But she loosened her hair in the casement. His face burnt like a brand
As the black cascade of perfume came tumbling over his breast;
And he kissed its waves in the moonlight,
    (O, sweet black waves in the moonlight!)
Then he tugged at his rein in the moonlight, and galloped away to the west.

PART TWO

He did not come in the dawning. He did not come at noon;
And out of the tawny sunset, before the rise of the moon,
When the road was a gypsy's ribbon, looping the purple moor,
A red-coat troop came marching—
    Marching—marching—
King George's men came marching, up to the old inn-door.

They said no word to the landlord. They drank his ale instead.
But they gagged his daughter, and bound her, to the foot of her narrow bed.
Two of them knelt at her casement, with muskets at their side!
There was death at every window;
    And hell at one dark window;
For Bess could see, through her casement, the road that *he* would ride.

They had tied her up to attention, with many a sniggering jest.
They had bound a musket beside her, with the muzzle beneath her breast!
"Now, keep good watch!" and they kissed her. She heard the doomed man say—
Look for me by moonlight;
    Watch for me by moonlight;
I'll come to thee by moonlight, though hell should bar the way!

She twisted her hands behind her; but all the knots held good!
She writhed her hands till her fingers were wet with sweat or blood!
They stretched and strained in the darkness, and the hours crawled by like years
Till, now, on the stroke of midnight,
    Cold, on the stroke of midnight,
The tip of one finger touched it! The trigger at least was hers!

The tip of one finger touched it. She strove no more for the rest.
Up, she stood up to attention, with the muzzle beneath her breast.
She would not risk their hearing; she would not strive again;
For the road lay bare in the moonlight;
    Blank and bare in the moonlight;
And the blood of her veins, in the moonlight, throbbed to her love's refrain.

Tlot-tlot; tlot-tlot! Had they heard it? The horse hoofs ringing clear;
Tlot-tlot; tlot-tlot, in the distance? Were they deaf that they did not hear?
Down the ribbon of moonlight, over the brow of the hill,
The highwayman came riding—
    Riding—riding—
The red coats looked to their priming! She stood up, straight and still.

Tlot-tlot, in the frosty silence! *Tlot-tlot,* in the echoing night!
Nearer he came and nearer. Her face was like a light.
Her eyes grew wide for a moment; she drew one last deep breath,
Then her finger moved in the moonlight,
    Her musket shattered the moonlight,
Shattered her breast in the moonlight and warned him—with her death.

He turned. He spurred to the west; he did not know who stood
Bowed, with her head o'er the musket, drenched with her own blood!
Not till the dawn he heard it, and his face grew grey to hear
How Bess, the landlord's daughter,
    The landlord's black-eyed daughter,
Had watched for her love in the moonlight, and died in the darkness there.

Back, he spurred like a madman, shrieking a curse to the sky,
With the white road smoking behind him and his rapier brandished high.
Blood red were his spurs in the golden noon; wine-red was his velvet coat;
When they shot him down on the highway,
    Down like a dog on the highway,
And he lay in his blood on the highway, with a bunch of lace at his throat.

And still of a winter's night, they say, when the wind is in the trees,
When the moon is a ghostly galleon tossed upon cloudy seas,
When the road is a ribbon of moonlight over the purple moor,
A highwayman comes riding—
    Riding—riding—
A highwayman comes riding, up to the old inn-door.

Over the cobbles he clatters and clangs in the dark inn-yard.
He taps with his whip on the shutters, but all is locked and barred.
He whistles a tune to the window, and who should be waiting there
But the landlord's black-eyed daughter,
    Bess, the landlord's daughter,
Plaiting a dark red love-knot into her long black hair.

John G. Saxe (1816–1869) worked as an attorney and became well-known as a public speaker who ran for governor twice but was defeated. Concerned about the hardening of the extremism that was leading the nation to civil war, he wrote "The Blind Men and the Elephant," which became his most famous poem. Our class learned this poem during a physics Main Lesson block to try to illustrate to the students the dangers of drawing conclusions from limited perceptions. This poem lends itself well to dramatic performance at an assembly. Note: some editions of this poem do not include the last stanza.

The Blind Men and the Elephant
John G. Saxe

It was six men of Indostan
To learning much inclined,
Who went to see the elephant
(Though all of them were blind),
That each by observation
Might satisfy his mind.

The first approached the elephant,
And, happening to fall
Against his broad and sturdy side,
At once began to bawl,
"God bless me! but the elephant
Is very like a wall!"

The second feeling of the tusk
Cried: "Ho! what have we here
So very round and smooth and sharp?
To me 'tis mighty clear
This wonder of an elephant
Is very like a spear!"

The third approached the animal,
And, happening to take
The squirming trunk within his hands
Thus boldly up and spake:
"I see," quoth he, "the elephant
Is very like a snake!"

The fourth reached out his eager hand
And felt about the knee;
"What most this wondrous beast is like
Is mighty plain," quoth he;
"'Tis clear enough the elephant
Is very like a tree."

The fifth, who chanced to touch the ear,
Said: "E'en the blindest man
Can tell what this resembles most,
Deny the fact who can,
This marvel of an elephant
Is very like a fan!"

The sixth no sooner had begun
About the beast to grope,
Than, seizing on the swinging tail
That fell within his scope,
"I see," quoth he, "the elephant
Is very like a rope!"

And so these men of Indostan
Disputed loud and long
Each in his own opinion
Exceeding stiff and strong,
Though each was partly in the right,
And all were in the wrong!

So, oft in theologic wars,
The disputants, I ween,
Tread on in utter ignorance,
Of what each other mean,
And prate about the elephant,
Not one of them has seen!

SPEECH EXERCISES

Seventh graders enjoy working on speech exercises in parts because they help them experience themselves as a multi-faceted group. Almost all speech exercises can be done with accompaniments; most can be done as rounds; and some can be turned into quodlibets.

For a special challenge, students can recite a quodlibet that is composed of alternating lines of two poems, i.e., the first line from the first poem followed by the second from the second poem, etc. For an even greater challenge, have them turn the quodlibet into a round using the alternating lines. Instructions for working with these variations are found on pages 34, 65–68, and 101–103. The following two poems use homonyms to challenge the listener. Make sure that the students are clear about the meaning of each homonym.

The Bear and the Boar

Once upon a barren moor
There dwelt a bear, also a boar;
The bear could not bear the boar,
The boar thought the bear a bore.
At last the boar could bear no more
The bear that bored him on the moor,
And so one morn he bored the bear;
That bear will bore the boar no more.

"Tree for Two" is well suited to be performed with dramatic gestures.

Tree for Two

A tree toad loved a she toad
That lived up in a tree.
She was a three-toed tree toad
But a two-toed toad was he.
The tree toad tried to win
The she toad's friendly nod,
For the tree toad loved the ground
On which the she toad trod.
But no matter how the two-toed tree toad tried
He could not please her whim;
In her tree toad bower
With her three-toed power
The she toad vetoed him.

"A Proper Cup of Coffee" is fun to recite with a British accent.

A Proper Cup of Coffee

All I want
Is a proper cup of coffee
Made in a proper copper coffeepot.
Tin pots or iron pots
They're no use to me.
If I can't have
A proper cup of coffee
Made in a proper copper coffeepot
I'll have a cup of tea.

Theodore Seuss Geisel (1904–1991), was an internationally-acclaimed author and illustrator, who published over 60 children's books under the pen name of Dr. Seuss. Many of his poems are suitable for recitation or can be used as speech exercises.

The Grip-top Sock
Dr. Seuss

Give me the gift of a grip-top sock,
A clip drape shipshape tip top sock.
Not your spinslick slapstick slipshod stock;
But a plastic, elastic grip-top sock.
None of your fantastic slack swap slop
From a slap dash flash cash haberdash shop.
Not a knick knack knitlock knockkneed knickerbocker sock
With a mock-shot blob-mottled trick-ticker top clock.
Not a supersheet seersucker ruck sack sock,
Not a spot-speckled frog-freckled cheap sheik's sock
Off a hodge-podge moss-blotched scotch-botched block.
Nothing slipshod drip drop flip flop or glip glop
Tip me to a tip top grip top sock.

The next three poems work particularly well with accompaniments or recited as rounds. Students can make suggestions for the accompaniments, and the class can determine which ones work best. When creating polyphonic compositions, it is important to keep them simple enough so that the density of words and sounds don't mask the meaning.

The Little Metal Kettle

There's a little metal kettle
That is sitting near the settle,
You can hear the tittle-tattle
Of the lid begin to rattle
When the kettle starts to boil.

What a pretty prittle-prattle
Of the kettle near the settle!
What a merry tittle-tattle
When the lid begins to rattle
And the kettle starts to boil.

The Night Light

There's no need to light a night light
On a light night like tonight,
For a night light's but a slight light,
And tonight's a night that's light.

Yes, tonight's light is a bright light,
So it's really not quite right
To light a night light with its slight light
On a light night like tonight.

Whether the Weather

Whether the weather be fine, or
    whether the weather be not;
Whether the weather be cold, or
    whether the weather be hot;
Whatever the weather,
We'll weather the weather,
Whether we like it or not.

Superlatives

Good, better, best
Never let it rest
Until your good is better
And your better best.

The next three poems work well together as quodlibets.

Out of his hole to steal he stole
A bag of chink he chunk.
And many a wicked smile he smole
And many a wink he wunk.

Amidst the mists and coldest frosts,
With barest wrists and stoutest boasts,
He thrusts his fists against the posts
And still insists he sees the ghosts.

Sheila Shorter sought a suitor;
Sheila sought a suitor short.
Sheila's suitor's sure to suit her;
Short's the suitor Sheila sought.

"How Much Wood Would a Woodchuck Chuck?" was the first polyphonic speech exercise that I composed as a young teacher. I decided to create additional parts that corresponded to three of the temperaments: Part 1 is the melancholic woodchuck; Part 2 is the sanguine woodchuck; and Part 3 is the choleric father or mother woodchuck who draws out the word "chuck" to rally their children. (I didn't include a phlegmatic woodchuck because I figured that it would probably not be interested in joining in the activity.)

You can perform the original speech exercise as a round and/or bring in the other parts. If you perform it, have students recite each part first so that the audience understands what is being said. Then have one group say the original exercise; bring in the first part after they've done it once; bring in the second part after they have done it twice, etc.

How Much Wood Would a Woodchuck Chuck?

How much wood would a woodchuck chuck
If a woodchuck could chuck wood?
It would chuck as much wood as a woodchuck could
If a woodchuck could chuck wood!

Additional parts:
1. Oh how I'm getting tired,
   Tired of chucking wood
   Oh how I'm getting tired,
   Of chucking so much wood.

2. I like chucking wood
   Chucking wood all day!
   I like chucking wood
   'Cause chucking wood's not work, it's play!

3. Chu—uck that wood!
   Come and chuck some wood!
   Chu—uck that wood!
   Come on, kids, let's chuck some wood!

Students will enjoy learning variations on "How Much Wood Would a Woodchuck Chuck?" such as the two included below. They can also be challenged to create their own. Learning about kennings can help generate ideas.

Kennings are compound words or word pairs that function like a simile or metaphor. Kennings were widely used by Old Norse and Old English poets, but they can be found in modern English as well. For example, the word "skyscraper," expresses a building's height by evoking the image of it scraping the sky. This can be applied as follows: "How much sky could a skyscraper scrape if a skyscraper could scrape sky?" Some other examples of modern kennings include: fender-bender, pencil-pusher, or tree-hugger.

How much ground could a groundhog hog
If a groundhog could hog ground?
It would hog as much ground as that groundhog found
If a groundhog could hog ground.

How much hair could a hair net net
If a hair net could net hair?
It would net as much hair
As the net could bear
If a hair net could net hair.

Here is a good exercise to recite dramatically:

Oh, the sadness of her sadness when she's sad.
Oh, the gladness of her gladness when she's glad.
But the sadness of her sadness,
and the gladness of her gladness,
Are nothing like her madness when she's mad!

TONGUE TWISTERS

Tongue twisters are fun to learn and can be challenging in terms of articulation and/or speed. As an additional challenge, you can require the students to practice fast recall in the learning process. It is important not to let tongue twisters get stale because your students lose interest and their speech will become sloppy. I therefore suggest working on a group of tongue twisters for a few days and then bringing in new ones. When students have become adept at reciting the week's tongue twisters, challenge them to recite them backwards. Other ideas of how to work with tongue twisters are included on pages 38–41, 69–75, and 152-154.[6]

The aged judge urges the jolly jury to be just but generous.

A bloke's back brake block broke
The broken brake block's in the back
It's a broken back brake block.

Blows the bitter blast, binds the barren bough,
Bud and blossom past—black is winter's brow.

Borachio Mustachio Whisterifustikus, the brave Bombadino of Baghdad helped Abomalique Bluebeard Bashow beat an abominable bumblebee at Balsora.

---

6 Additional tongue twisters can be found at the ends of the chapters for 5th, 6th, and 8th Grades.

Collectible classics cause considerable consternation among auto aficionados.

Conrad came careering round the corner
Completing his crazy career by crashing into the crypt.

The following exercise in English corresponds to one by Rudolf Steiner in German. In addition to adding words, it features the pure vowel sounds of *a, e, o,* and *u* which are created ever further back in the mouth. Other speech exercises by Rudolf Steiner can be worked with, but I suggest that you ask a speech artist to coach you to do them properly.

Dart
Dart saves
Dart saves dear
Dart saves dear loan
Dart saves dear loan through
Dart saves dear loan through darkening
Dart saves dear loan through darkening loading

Dashing dangerously down the dale,
Dainty Dinah dashed dizzily past Dorothy.

Don't pamper damp scamp tramps that camp under ramp lamps.

The drain in the train dripped again and again until the drain in the train dripped dry.

Five fashionable females flying to France for fresh fashions.

George Gabs grabs crabs,
Crabs George Gabs grabs.
If George Gabs grabs crabs
Where are the crabs George grabs?

Lesser leather never weathered wetter weather better.
Wetter weather never weathered lesser leather less.

Maud walked on the lawn, Paul crawled along the wall.
Maud called to Paul, "You'll fall!" "Not at all!" called Paul.

Men munch much mush.
Women munch much mush.
Many men and women must munch much mush.

Mixed metaphors muddle middling minds.

Mr. Knox keeps his socks
In a pale pink chocolate-box—
Orange socks with spots and clocks.

Mother's mellow miracle mustard makes most moldy meat much more munchable.

Your imbecilic mimicking is sickening.

Oh Horace! Isn't it horrible when you're hot and in a hurry and you've got to hold your hat in your hand?

Please Paul, pause for applause.
Pause for applause, Paul.

Peter has five prize pigs pirouetting perpetually in the poppies.

Palatable prescriptions properly prescribed please paying patients.

If practice makes perfect and perfect needs practice,
I'm perfectly practiced and practically perfect.

She let little Nellie run a little but told her:
"Don't run along the wrong lane."

Several exceptionally technical secretaries at separate tables
Equitably separating economics textbooks.

Please sell me some short silk socks and some shimmering satin sashes.

She saw the shiny soapy suds
Sailing down the shallow sink.

The seething sea ceaseth and thus the seething sea sufficeth us.

I'm a sheet slitter. I slit sheets.
I'm the sleekest sheet slitter that ever slit sheets.

I sit and slit and slit and sit; upon the slitted sheet I sit.

I shot the city sheriff. I shot the city sheriff. I shot the city sheriff.

If neither he sells seashells
Nor she sells seashells,
Who shall sell seashells
If seashells be sold?

She stops at the shops where I shop
And if she shops at the shops where I shop
I won't stop at the shop where she shops.

Sheep shouldn't sleep in a shack;
Sheep should sleep in a shed.

Sheila uttered a sharp shrill shriek
and shrunk from the shriveled form
that slumbered in the shadows.

Shut up the shutters and sit in the shop!

Six sick hicks nick six slick bricks with picks and sticks.

Some seventy-six sad seasick seamen soon set sail,
seeking soothing salty South Sea sunshine.

She stood on the balcony inexplicably mimicking him hiccupping and amicably welcoming him in.

Something whistled past his head;
A miss again!" his Missus said
Something struck him in the ear.
"I don't miss twice, now do I, dear?"

Ten tiny toddling tots trying to train their tongues to trill.

The squire squealed with breathalyzing indignation quaveringly, splutter complete repudiation of the impossibly preposterous allegation of gross intoxication.

The suitability of a suet pudding without superfluous plums is a superstition presumably due to Susan's true economy.

This is the catastrophic hypothesis of the suppositious apothecary.

Till Tom taught tact to Tim, Tim talked trash to tots.

I thought a thought.
But the thought I thought wasn't the thought I thought I thought.
If the thought I thought I thought had been the thought I thought, I wouldn't have though so much.

Top chopstick shops stock top chopsticks,
While cheap chop suey shops stock cheap soup chips.

The unusual confusion surrounding the revision of the decision regarding the seizure and closure of the garage is surely due to some measure of confusion.

Vivid, virtuous, vast and void; never be victim to villainous vices.

Where ignorance predominates—
Vulgarity invariably asserts itself.

Wiles and snares and snares and wiles of a snary, wily world.

Why is the worst verse worse than the first verse?

Recitation in Eighth Grade

Eighth graders are deeply interested in questions about the world as well as in questions of the identity and relationships. The eighth grade curriculum addresses these interests through the study of modern history and the physical sciences, which help students to connect to their world; and through the study of literature physiology, and geography, which help them deepen their sense of self and their understanding of others.

Recitation reinforces the subjects that the students study and it also gives them a glimpse of the complexity and challenges of the human experience. Because you have wide latitude in choosing poems and prose passages to recite and read, I encourage you choose selections based on what you think your students need and will respond to. In previous chapters I grouped selections by theme; in this chapter, I have arranged them chronologically to give you a better sense of their historical context.

For the study of history, students can be introduced to the ideas and the ideals of our nation's founding. Some of our nation's founding documents can be read and studied, and students can memorize relevant sections. Learning part of the Declaration of Independence, the Preamble to the Constitution, or the Gettysburg Address fosters a life-long connection to these works. When your students are older and encounter these documents again, the words they learned and recited will resonate deep within them.

For the study of social activism, rights, and social justice, students can work on selections from writers who awaken a sense of identity and social responsibility. My students have responded well to Walt Whitman's "O Captain, My Captain!," to Dr. Martin Luther King's "I Have a Dream" speech and to Chief Seattle's letter expressing the Native Americans' relationship to the land. I encourage you to find other selections that speak to your students' interests and ideals.

Because there is a limit to what the whole class can learn or read together, longer recitations can be divided among individuals or assigned to groups. I also suggest that you have your students find and share poems and prose works that they find meaningful by compiling them into an anthology that can be used for recitation selections or for discussion topics.

By eighth grade, your students will have become more competent in their speech. Now is the time to stretch their abilities by having them learn more difficult works and perform them with greater expression and more nuanced timing. Tongue twisters can continue to be used as warm-up exercises, and your students may enjoy revisiting some of speech rounds and polyphonic pieces that they learned in earlier grades, but these should not detract from the time needed to learn the recitations. Instructions for variations for working with speech are provided in the fifth-grade chapter.

Morning Exercises in eighth grade no longer need to be coordinated with the Main Lesson blocks, though when it's possible to create routines that last for four weeks, it will help the students master the recitations. Works that do not need to be worked on for a the whole block can be replaced by new selections.

Before beginning to work on a recitation, you should introduce it. Recitations about curricular subjects need no introduction, because the Main Lesson presentation will have provided the context. For all other selections, introductions should include the title and the author of the work, and, if you wish, something about the author's life and the work's background and context.

Next you should provide a brief summary of the work and speak about the important themes, people, or events. If the form and style of the work are important, they should be mentioned, and if any literary devices are used, they should be highlighted.

Introductions to works with particularly meaningful themes, characters, or events should include your comments. I encourage you to express your opinion freely because your students will learn a great deal, not only about the recitation, but about you. Introductions to important works can also include a class discussion that explores the work's importance and relevance. These discussions strengthen the class community as the students get to know each other better, and they deepen our bond with our students as we express what we think and believe.

What has been described all occurs *before* students hear the work for the first time. This approach may seem counter-intuitive because we typically discuss and analyze a work *after* we have heard it. But this approach appeals to the students' feelings, especially to their curiosity and interest. And when they hear the work for the first time, students will connect with the work more completely, understand more it deeply, and appreciate it more fully.

If you wish to learn more about this novel approach, please refer to Discussion 6 of *Discussions with Teachers*, where Rudolf Steiner demonstrated how a teacher might introduce a fable or a poem. If you are new to this method, I encourage you to try it. Although you may feel a bit awkward at first, I believe that you will quickly experience how well it works.

By eighth grade, students should be very adept at learning and memorizing selections. After working on a selection for a while, students should be expected to recite it individually. This gives them—and you—an opportunity to see if they have truly learned it, and it helps prepare them for public speaking. When it is time for individual recitations, I suggest that the class recite the work first. Then those who are most capable and confident can volunteer to recite individually. Those who need more time will benefit from listening and reciting the selection inwardly while it is being spoken.

Morning Exercises help students to put aside their everyday lives and begin to focus on the demands of the school day. They should not exceed 20–25 minutes per day, however, because when they are too long, students can become less attentive and responsive, and they may have difficulty concentrating on their work. Morning Exercises are important, but we need to remember that they are only a preparation for—not a major component of—the Main Lesson.[7]

YEARLY VERSES

Verses that are recited throughout the year have a special place in the speech curriculum. The daily repetition of these verses imprints them in the students' hearts and affirms life-long ideals. Because a verse that is recited daily can end up being done without much thought, I recommend occasionally bringing it to consciousness occasionally by discussing the meaning and importance of the theme or a special phrase, and/or using it as a writing prompt.

A typical eighth-grade Main Lesson might begin with announcements, class housekeeping, and/or a check-in. I think that these should all precede the recitation of the Morning Verse so that it can mark the formal beginning of the Main Lesson. If possible, all the upper grades in your school should use the same version of the verse because this builds a sense of community among the classes. I have therefore not included versions of the Morning Verse because it is important for each school to choose the one they prefer.

My students recited the following verses all year long: the Morning Verse at the beginning of Main Lesson; "There Lives in Me an Image" at the end of the Morning Exercises; "May Wisdom Shine through Me" at the end of the Main Lesson; and "At the Ringing of the Bells" at the end of the day.

Angelus Silesius (1624–1677) was the name that Johann Scheffler adopted when he became a Catholic priest, and he composed many religious poems that expressed his mystical beliefs. My students and I recited "There Lives in Me an Image" for all eight years of our journey together because I hoped that it would become a motto for their lives.

There Lives in Me an Image
Angelus Silesius

There lives in me an image,
Of all that I should be;
Until I have become it,
My heart is never free.

---

[7] Suggestions for creating Morning Exercises may be found at the end of this chapter.

May Wisdom Shine through Me
Rudolf Steiner

May wisdom shine through me,
May love glow within me,
May strength permeate me,
That in me may arise
A helper of humankind,
A server of holy things,
Selfless and true.

At the Ringing of the Bells
Rudolf Steiner

To wonder at beauty,
Stand guard over truth,
Look up to the noble,
Decide for the good—
Leads us on our journey
To goals for our life:
To right in our doing;
To peace in our feeling;
To light in our thought.
And teaches us trust
In the guidance of God;
In all that there is—
In the world-wide All,
In the soul's deep soil.

POETRY AND PROSE SELECTIONS (in chronological order)

Eighth graders benefit from reading and reciting poetry and prose that express the work of the divine in the world and reassure them that they are not alone. If you are going to use excerpts from the Bible, you need to have a relationship to them. Students will sense that relationship and will appreciate the opportunity to get to know you better by sensing your values.

I recommend a section of Paul's "Letter to the Corinthians" because it is such a poignant expression of the qualities of love. In your introduction, you might briefly tell the students about St. Paul, and how he was transformed by a direct encounter with Christ. Your introduction might also include a conversation about love and how it expresses itself.

Letter to the Corinthians (excerpt)
St. Paul

Though I speak with the tongues of men and of angels, and have not love, I am become as sounding brass, or a tinkling cymbal.
And though I have the gift of prophecy, and understand all mysteries, and all knowledge; and though I have all faith, so that I could remove mountains, and have not love, I am nothing....
Love suffereth long, and is kind; love envieth not; love vaunteth not itself, is not puffed up,
Doth not behave itself unseemly, seeketh not her own, is not easily provoked, thinketh no evil;
Rejoiceth not in iniquity, but rejoiceth in the truth;
Beareth all things, believeth all things, hopeth all things, endureth all things....
When I was a child, I spake as a child, I understood as a child, I thought as a child: but when I became a man, I put away childish things.
For now we see through a glass, darkly; but then face to face: now I know in part; but then shall I know even as also I am known.
And now abideth faith, hope, love, these three; but the greatest of these is love.

Students will probably encounter the 23rd Psalm at many points in their lives. If they memorize it in eighth grade, it will resonate whenever they hear it again. Your introduction might include a conversation about the kinds of circumstances that compel people to seek for divine guidance and reassurance.

23rd Psalm
A Psalm of David

The Lord is my Shepherd; I shall not want.
He maketh me to lie down in green pastures:
He leadeth me beside the still waters.
He restoreth my soul: He leadeth me in the paths of righteousness
    for His name' sake.
Yea, though I walk through the valley of the shadow of death,
I will fear no evil: For thou art with me;
Thy rod and thy staff, they comfort me.
Thou preparest a table before me in the presence of mine enemies;
Thou annointest my head with oil; My cup runneth over.
Surely goodness and mercy shall follow me all the days of my life,
    and I will dwell in the House of the Lord forever.

This well-known passage from Ecclesiastes is also worth reading or reciting. Because the recitation presents polarities, it benefits from being recited in pairs or in groups.

To Every Thing There Is a Season
Ecclesiastes 3:1-8

To every thing there is a season, and a time to every purpose under the heaven:
A time to be born, a time to die; a time to plant, and a time to pluck up that
   which is planted;
A time to kill, and a time to heal; a time to break down, and a time to build up;
A time to weep, and a time to laugh; a time to mourn, and a time to dance;
A time to cast away stones, and a time to gather stones together; a time to
   embrace, and a time to refrain from embracing;
A time to get, and a time to lose; a time to keep, and a time to cast away;
A time to rend, and a time to sew; a time to keep silence, and a time to speak;
A time to love, and a time to hate; a time of war, and a time of peace.

In many Waldorf schools, William Shakespeare (1564–1616) holds a special place in eighth grade because they perform a Shakespeare play. Such a production requires a commitment to mastering Shakespeare's language. This commitment will bear fruit because Shakespeare's language transforms the students' speech. If you decide not to do a play by Shakespeare, students can still learn several memorable speeches from Shakespeare's plays such as these:

This England
William Shakespeare
from Richard II

This royal throne of kings, this scepter'd isle,
This earth of majesty, this seat of Mars,
This other Eden, demi-paradise,
This fortress built by Nature for herself
Against infection and the hand of war,
This happy breed of men, this little world,
This precious stone set in the silver sea
Which serves it in the office of a wall,
Or as a moat defensive to a house,
Against the envy of less happier lands,
This blessed plot, this earth, this realm, this England.

The Quality of Mercy
William Shakespeare
from *The Merchant of Venice*

The quality of mercy is not strain'd,
It droppeth as the gentle rain from heaven
Upon the place beneath: it is twice blest;
It blesseth him that gives and him that takes:
'Tis mightiest in the mightiest: it becomes
The throned monarch better than his crown;
His sceptre shows the force of temporal power,
The attribute to awe and majesty,
Wherein doth sit the dread and fear of kings;
But mercy is above this sceptred sway;
It is enthroned in the hearts of kings,
It is an attribute to God himself;
And earthly power doth then show likest God's
When mercy seasons justice.

Tomorrow, and tomorrow, and tomorrow
William Shakespeare
from *Macbeth*

Tomorrow, and tomorrow, and tomorrow,
Creeps in this petty pace from day to day,
To the last syllable of recorded time;
And all our yesterdays have lighted fools
The way to dusty death. Out, out, brief candle!
Life's but a walking shadow, a poor player,
That struts and frets his hour upon the stage,
And then is heard no more. It is a tale
Told by an idiot, full of sound and fury,
Signifying nothing.

To Thine Own Self Be True
William Shakespeare
from *Hamlet*

This above all: to thine own self be true,
And it must follow, as the night the day,
Thou canst not then be false to any man.

Shakespeare's sonnets are also worth learning. In the beginning of eighth grade, I gave each student a volume of Shakespeare's sonnets and told them to find one that they could recite as their birthday verse for the year. Hearing several sonnets each day imprinted them in the students' memories and will be a gift for life. I recommend choosing several sonnets to recite as a class. Here are two to consider:

Sonnet 18
William Shakespeare

Shall I compare thee to a summer's day?
Thou art more lovely and more temperate.
Rough winds do shake the darling buds of May,
And summer's lease hath all too short a date.
Sometime too hot the eye of heaven shines,
And often is his gold complexion dimmed;
And every fair from fair sometime declines,
By chance, or nature's changing course, untrimmed;
But thy eternal summer shall not fade,
Nor lose possession of that fair thou ow'st,
Nor shall death brag thou wand'rest in his shade,
When in eternal lines to Time thou grow'st.
   So long as men can breathe, or eyes can see,
   So long lives this, and this gives life to thee.

Sonnet 29
William Shakespeare

When, in disgrace with fortune and men's eyes,
I all alone beweep my outcast state,
And trouble deaf heaven with my bootless cries,
And look upon myself and curse my fate,
Wishing me like to one more rich in hope,
Featured like him, like him with friends possessed,
Desiring this man's art and that man's scope,
With what I most enjoy contented least;
Yet in these thoughts myself almost despising,
Haply I think on thee, and then my state,
(Like to the lark at break of day arising
From sullen earth) sings hymns at heaven's gate;
   For thy sweet love remembered such wealth brings
   That then I scorn to change my state with kings.

John Donne's Meditation "No Man (One) Is an Island" expresses the recognition that each of us is related to everyone else. John Donne (1572–1641) was a poet and scholar, who served as a member of parliament and as a clergyman. In 1623, John Donne almost died from an illness, and when he recovered, he wrote a series of meditations on health and illness, pain and death. Like much of Donne's poetry, this Meditation uses the rhythms of everyday speech.

Your introduction might include a conversation about the central metaphor of this poem and you and your students can explore what it means to be involved in humankind.

Editor's Note: "man" in the original has been changed to "one," and "mankind" to "humankind."

Meditation (1624)
John Donne

No one is an island entire of itself; everyone is a piece of the continent,
a part of the main; if a clod be washed away by the sea, Europe is the less,
as well as if a promontory were, as well as a manor of thy friends or of thine
own were; anyone's death diminishes me, because I am involved in humankind.
And therefore never send to know for whom the bell tolls; it tolls for thee.

Students' sense of meaning in life is strengthened by deepening their connection to their community, their heritage, and their country. The study of modern history and current events aids this process.

As Americans studying civics, your students should be introduced to the ideas and ideals of our nation's founding documents. Learning part of the Declaration of Independence or the Preamble to the Constitution by heart fosters a life-long connection to these works. When students are older and encounter these documents again, the words they memorized will resonate deep within them.

If these documents were included in your presentation during Main Lesson, they need no introduction. I suggest, however, that plenty of time be reserved to discuss, and perhaps write about, their content, meaning, and relevance.

The Beginning of The Declaration of Independence (1776)

When in the Course of human events, it becomes necessary for one people to dissolve the political bands which have connected them with another, and to assume among the powers of the earth, the separate and equal station to which the Laws of Nature and of Nature's God entitle them, a decent respect to the opinions of mankind requires that they should declare the causes which impel them to the separation.

We hold these truths to be self-evident, that all men are created equal, that they are endowed by their Creator with certain unalienable Rights, that among these are Life, Liberty and the pursuit of Happiness.—That to secure these rights, Governments are instituted among Men, deriving their just powers from the consent of the governed,—That whenever any Form of Government becomes destructive of these ends, it is the Right of the People to alter or to abolish it, and to institute new Government, laying its foundation on such principles and organizing its powers in such form, as to them shall seem most likely to effect their Safety and Happiness.

Preamble to the Constitution (1787)

We the People of the United States, in Order to form a more perfect Union, establish Justice, insure domestic Tranquility, provide for the common defence, promote the general Welfare, and secure the Blessings of Liberty to ourselves and our Posterity, do ordain and establish this Constitution for the United States of America.

Samuel Taylor Coleridge (1772–1834) was an English Romantic poet. "Rime of the Ancient Mariner" first appeared in a volume that featured poetry by Coleridge and his friend, William Wordsworth. Coleridge faced health challenges all his life, and as an adult he suffered from crippling bouts of anxiety and depression.

Your introduction could include a summary of the entire poem so that the students understand the context for this selection. Once the students have begun working on the recitation, it would be interesting to explore the poem's setting and to consider the characters of the mariner and the albatross in light of Coleridge's health challenges.

Rime of the Ancient Mariner (1798) (excerpt)
Samuel Taylor Coleridge

And now the STORM-BLAST came, and he
Was tyrannous and strong:
He struck with his o'ertaking wings,
And chased us south along.

With sloping masts and dipping prow,
As who pursued with yell and blow
Still treads the shadow of his foe,
And forward bends his head,
The ship drove fast, loud roared the blast,
And southward aye we fled.

And now there came both mist and snow,
And it grew wondrous cold:
And ice, mast-high, came floating by,
As green as emerald.

And through the drifts the snowy clifts
Did send a dismal sheen:
Nor shapes of men nor beasts we ken—
The ice was all between.

The ice was here, the ice was there,
The ice was all around:
It cracked and growled, and roared and howled,
Like noises in a swound!

At length did cross an Albatross,
Thorough the fog it came;
As if it had been a Christian soul,
We hailed it in God's name.

It ate the food it ne'er had eat,
And round and round it flew.
The ice did split with a thunder-fit;
The helmsman steered us through!

And a good south wind sprung up behind;
The Albatross did follow,
And every day, for food or play,
Came to the mariner's hollo!

In mist or cloud, on mast or shroud,
It perched for vespers nine;
Whiles all the night, through fog-smoke white,
Glimmered the white Moon-shine.

'God save thee, ancient Mariner!
From the fiends, that plague thee thus!—
Why look'st thou so?'—With my cross-bow
I shot the ALBATROSS.

"A Visit from St. Nicholas" was first published anonymously, but once it became well-known, Clement Clarke Moore (1779–1863) claimed authorship, though some scholars attribute the poem to Henry Livingston Jr.

In your introduction, you might ask the students what remember about Saint Nicholas's life if they heard about him in second grade. The name "Santa Claus" evolved from Dutch name for Saint Nicholas, which is "Sinterklass." You might also let them know how many of the details of this poem have entered popular culture: the sleigh drawn by reindeer; the descent down the chimney with stockings hanging from the mantle; and St. Nicholas's appearance and clothing.

A Visit from St. Nicholas (1823)
Clement Clarke Moore or Henry Livingston Jr.

'Twas the night before Christmas, when all through the house
Not a creature was stirring, not even a mouse;
The stockings were hung by the chimney with care,
In hopes that St. Nicholas soon would be there;
The children were nestled all snug in their beds,
While visions of sugar-plums danced in their heads;
And mamma in her 'kerchief, and I in my cap,
Had just settled our brains for a long winter's nap,
When out on the lawn there arose such a clatter,
I sprang from the bed to see what was the matter.
Away to the window I flew like a flash,
Tore open the shutters and threw up the sash.
The moon on the breast of the new-fallen snow
Gave the lustre of mid-day to objects below,
When, what to my wondering eyes should appear,
But a miniature sleigh, and eight tiny reindeer,
With a little old driver, so lively and quick,
I knew in a moment it must be St. Nick.
More rapid than eagles his coursers they came,
And he whistled, and shouted, and called them by name;
"Now, Dasher! now, Dancer! now, Prancer and Vixen!
On, Comet! on, Cupid! on, Donder and Blitzen!
To the top of the porch! to the top of the wall!
Now dash away! dash away! dash away all!"
As dry leaves that before the wild hurricane fly,
When they meet with an obstacle, mount to the sky;
So up to the house-top the coursers they flew,
With the sleigh full of toys, and St. Nicholas too.
And then, in a twinkling, I heard on the roof
The prancing and pawing of each little hoof.
As I drew in my head, and was turning around,
Down the chimney St. Nicholas came with a bound.
He was dressed all in fur, from his head to his foot,
And his clothes were all tarnished with ashes and soot;
A bundle of Toys he had flung on his back,
And he looked like a pedler just opening his pack.
His eyes—how they twinkled! his dimples how merry!
His cheeks were like roses, his nose like a cherry!
His droll little mouth was drawn up like a bow
And the beard of his chin was as white as the snow;
The stump of a pipe he held tight in his teeth,
And the smoke it encircled his head like a wreath;
He had a broad face and a little round belly,
That shook when he laughed, like a bowlful of jelly.

He was chubby and plump, a right jolly old elf,
And I laughed when I saw him, in spite of myself;
A wink of his eye and a twist of his head,
Soon gave me to know I had nothing to dread;
He spoke not a word, but went straight to his work,
And filled all the stockings; then turned with a jerk,
And laying his finger aside of his nose,
And giving a nod, up the chimney he rose;
He sprang to his sleigh, to his team gave a whistle,
And away they all flew like the down of a thistle,
But I heard him exclaim, ere he drove out of sight,
"Happy Christmas to all, and to all a good-night."

Lydia Huntley Sigourney (1791–1865) was a popular American poet and writer who published over 50 books and hundreds of periodical articles. She was a role model for the women of her day, demonstrating that they could be successful and take up their rightful role in society. Lydia Sigourney condemned slavery and the injustices done to Native Americans, and she used her position and prominence to advocate for social reform.

Your introduction to this poem might explore its themes and images in light of the destruction of Native American culture. Students might enjoy the challenge of researching the Native American names that are mentioned.

Indian Names (1834)
Lydia Huntley Sigourney

'How can the red men be forgotten, while so many of our states and territories, bays, lakes, and rivers, are indelibly stamped by names of their giving?'

Ye say they all have passed away,
    That noble race and brave,
That their light canoes have vanished
    From off the crested wave;
That 'mid the forests where they roamed
    There rings no hunter shout,
But their name is on your waters,
    Ye may not wash it out.

'Tis where Ontario's billow
    Like Ocean's surge is curled,
Where strong Niagara's thunders wake
    The echo of the world.
Where red Missouri bringeth
    Rich tribute from the west,
And Rappahannock sweetly sleeps
    On green Virginia's breast.

Ye say their cone-like cabins,
  That clustered o'er the vale,
Have fled away like withered leaves
  Before the autumn gale,
But their memory liveth on your hills,
  Their baptism on your shore,
Your everlasting rivers speak
  Their dialect of yore.

Old Massachusetts wears it,
  Within her lordly crown,
And broad Ohio bears it,
  Amid his young renown;
Connecticut hath wreathed it
  Where her quiet foliage waves,
And bold Kentucky breathed it hoarse
  Through all her ancient caves.

Wachuset hides its lingering voice
  Within his rocky heart,
And Alleghany graves its tone
  Throughout his lofty chart;
Monadnock on his forehead hoar
  Doth seal the sacred trust,
Your mountains build their monument,
  Though ye destroy their dust.

Ye call these red-browned brethren
  The insects of an hour,
Crushed like the noteless worm amid
  The regions of their power;
Ye drive them from their father's lands,
  Ye break of faith the seal,
But can ye from the court of Heaven
  Exclude their last appeal?

Ye see their unresisting tribes,
  With toilsome step and slow,
On through the trackless desert pass
  A caravan of woe;
Think ye the Eternal's ear is deaf?
  His sleepless vision dim?
Think ye the *soul's blood* may not cry
  From that far land to him?

Ralph Waldo Emerson (1803–1882) was widely known in both Europe and America as a poet, philosopher, essayist, and lecturer. In your introduction, you might consider the theme of time and how memory redeems its inexorable passage. This poem could be learned when you teach about the buildup to the Civil War, and you could discuss how both North and South considered themselves the heirs of the founding impulse of independence.

Concord Hymn (1847)
Ralph Waldo Emerson

Sung at the Completion of the Battle Monument, July 4, 1837

By the rude bridge that arched the flood,
    Their flag to April's breeze unfurled,
Here once the embattled farmers stood
    And fired the shot heard round the world.

The foe long since in silence slept;
    Alike the conqueror silent sleeps;
And Time the ruined bridge has swept
    Down the dark stream which seaward creeps.

On this green bank, by this soft stream,
    We set today a votive stone;
That memory may their deed redeem,
    When, like our sires, our sons are gone.

Spirit, that made those heroes dare
    To die, and leave their children free,
Bid Time and Nature gently spare
    The shaft we raise to them and thee.

Chief Seattle (ca. 1786–1866) was a Suquamish and Duwamish chief who tried to reach an accommodation with the white settlers in western Washington state. In 1854 he gave a famous speech which was reconstructed and published many years later. The translation of this speech has gone through many versions, and this excerpt is one of the best-known.

This speech could be included in a presentation about the challenges facing the Native Americans during the expansion of the western frontier by white settlers. It could also be shared when considering environmental or social justice issues. Whether the speech is read or recited, it will stimulate meaningful discussions about different relationships to the land.

Speech by Chief Seattle (1854) (excerpt)

This we know: the earth does not belong to man, man belongs to the earth. All things are connected like the blood that unites us all. Man did not weave the web of life, he is merely a strand in it. Whatever he does to the web, he does it to himself. One thing we know: our god is also your god. The earth is precious to him and to harm the earth is to heap contempt on its creator.

Your destiny is a mystery to us. What will happen when the buffalo are all slaughtered? The wild horses tamed? What will happen when the secret corners of the forest are heavy with the scent of many men and the view of the ripe hills is blotted by talking wires? Where will the thicket be? Gone! Where will the eagle be? Gone! And what is it to say goodbye to the swift pony and the hunt? The end of living and the beginning of survival. When the last Red Man has vanished with this wilderness and his memory is only the shadow of a cloud moving across the prairie, will these shores and forests still be here? Will there be any of the spirit of my people left?

We love this earth as a newborn loves its mother's heartbeat. So, if we sell you our land, love it as we have loved it. Care for it as we have cared for it. Hold in your mind the memory of the land as it is when you receive it. Preserve the land for all children and love it, as God loves us all. As we are part of the land, you too are part of the land. This earth is precious to us. It is also precious to you. One thing we know: there is only one God. No man, be he Red Man or White Man, can be apart. We are brothers after all.

Alfred, Lord Tennyson (1809–1892) was the most famous English poet of the Victorian era. In this poem, Tennyson commemorates the charge of a brigade during the Crimean War when the light cavalry troopers pressed onwards in the face of inevitable death. When you introduce the poem, you might discuss the second stanza in light of quote from the newspaper article that inspired Tennyson to write the poem: "The British soldier will do his duty, even to certain death, and is not paralyzed by the feeling that he is the victim of some hideous blunder." This poem can serve as the basis for a conversation about the many types of duty.

The Charge of the Light Brigade (1854)
Alfred, Lord Tennyson

Half a league, half a league,
Half a league onward,
All in the valley of Death
   Rode the six hundred.
"Forward, the Light Brigade!
Charge for the guns!" he said.
Into the valley of Death
   Rode the six hundred.

"Forward, the Light Brigade!"
Was there a man dismayed?
Not though the soldier knew
   Someone had blundered.
   Theirs not to make reply,
   Theirs not to reason why,
   Theirs but to do and die.
   Into the valley of Death
   Rode the six hundred.

Cannon to right of them,
Cannon to left of them,
Cannon in front of them
   Volleyed and thundered;
Stormed at with shot and shell,
Boldly they rode and well,
Into the jaws of Death,
Into the mouth of hell
   Rode the six hundred.

Flashed all their sabres bare,
Flashed as they turned in air
Sabring the gunners there,
Charging an army, while
   All the world wondered.
Plunged in the battery-smoke
Right through the line they broke;
Cossack and Russian
Reeled from the sabre stroke
   Shattered and sundered.
Then they rode back, but not
   Not the six hundred.

Cannon to right of them,
Cannon to left of them,
Cannon behind them
   Volleyed and thundered;
Stormed at with shot and shell,
While horse and hero fell.
They that had fought so well
Came through the jaws of Death,
Back from the mouth of hell,
All that was left of them,
   Left of six hundred.

When can their glory fade?
O the wild charge they made!
   All the world wondered.
Honour the charge they made!
Honour the Light Brigade,
   Noble six hundred!

The Civil War and the life of Abraham Lincoln are some of the most important topics in your study of American History. By memorizing and reciting Lincoln's Gettysburg Address, students will absorb some of our nation's loftiest ideals. If you mention this address during your presentation of the life of Abraham Lincoln and the Civil War, you will not need to introduce it separately. This speech can elicit meaningful conversations and/or compositions about America's ideals, the meaning of "United States," and the inadequacy of war to bring about resolution to conflicts.

Gettysburg Address (1863)
Abraham Lincoln

Four score and seven years ago our fathers brought forth on this continent, a new nation, conceived in liberty, and dedicated to the proposition that all men are created equal.

Now we are engaged in a great civil war, testing whether that nation, or any nation so conceived and so dedicated can long endure. We are met on a great battle-field of that war. We have come to dedicate a portion of that field, as a final resting place for those who here gave their lives that that nation might live. It is altogether fitting and proper that we should do this.

But, in a larger sense, we can not dedicate—we can not consecrate—we can not hallow—this ground. The brave men, living and dead, who struggled here, have consecrated it, far above our poor power to add or detract. The world will little note, nor long remember what we say here, but it can never forget what they did here. It is for us the living, rather, to be dedicated here to the unfinished work which they who fought here have thus far so nobly advanced. It is rather for us to be here dedicated to the great task remaining before us—that from these honored dead we take increased devotion to that cause for which they gave the last full measure of devotion—that we here highly resolve that these dead shall not have died in vain—that this nation, under God, shall have a new birth of freedom—and that government of the people, by the people, for the people, shall not perish from the earth.

Walt Whitman (1919–1892) was a very influential American poet, who pioneered the use of free verse. During the Civil War, Walt Whitman moved to Washington, D.C., where he volunteered to work as a nurse. He greatly admired Abraham Lincoln and was moved by his death to write "O Captain, My Captain!"

This poem could be included in your presentation of the life of Abraham Lincoln. Before working on it, your introduction might include a review of what metaphors are. In your introduction, the metaphors and the power of repetition in the poem might be examined.

O Captain, My Captain (1865)
Walt Whitman

O Captain! my Captain! our fearful trip is done,
The ship has weather'd every rack, the prize we sought is won,
The port is near, the bells I hear, the people all exulting,
While follow eyes the steady keel, the vessel grim and daring;
    But O heart! heart! heart!
      O the bleeding drops of red,
        Where on the deck my Captain lies,
          Fallen cold and dead.

O Captain! my Captain! rise up and hear the bells;
Rise up—for you the flag is flung—for you the bugle trills,
For you bouquets and ribbon'd wreaths—for you the shores a-crowding,
For you they call, the swaying mass, their eager faces turning;
    Here Captain! dear father!
      This arm beneath your head!
        It is some dream that on the deck,
          You've fallen cold and dead.

My Captain does not answer, his lips are pale and still,
My father does not feel my arm, he has no pulse nor will,
The ship is anchor'd safe and sound, its voyage closed and done,
From fearful trip the victor ship comes in with object won;
    Exult O shores, and ring O bells!
      But I with mournful tread,
        Walk the deck my Captain lies,
          Fallen cold and dead.

William Ernest Henley (1849–1903) was an English poet, writer, and editor. When he was 16, he suffered complications from tuberculosis that required his left leg to be amputated. When he was told that his other leg needed to be amputated as well, he sought the care of the famous English surgeon Joseph Lister, who performed several operations and saved his leg. Henley wrote "Invictus" while recovering from these operations.

In your introduction, you might discuss the theme of this poem in light of Shakespeare's assertion "Sweet are the uses of adversity" and Friedrich Nietzsche's contention that "Whatever doesn't kill me makes me stronger." This poem also lends itself to an examination of symbols and metaphors.

Invictus (1875)
William Ernest Henley

Out of the night that covers me,
    Black as the pit from pole to pole,
I thank whatever gods may be
    For my unconquerable soul.

In the fell clutch of circumstance
    I have not winced nor cried aloud.
Under the bludgeonings of chance
    My head is bloody, but unbowed.

Beyond this place of wrath and tears
    Looms but the Horror of the shade,
And yet the menace of the years
    Finds and shall find me unafraid.

It matters not how strait the gate,
    How charged with punishments the scroll,
I am the master of my fate,
    I am the captain of my soul.

Gerard Manley Hopkins (1844–1889) is now considered to be one of the greatest poets of the Victorian era, though much of his poetry was not accepted for publication until after his death. Gerard Manley Hopkins was a Jesuit priest, and many of his poems reflect his view of the Divine.

In your introduction, you might consider the themes of captivity and freedom and compare this poem with Maya Angelou's "Caged Bird."

The Caged Skylark (1877)
Gerard Manley Hopkins

As a dare-gale skylark scanted in a dull cage,
   Man's mounting spirit in his bone-house, mean house, dwells —
   That bird beyond the remembering his free fells;
This in drudgery, day-laboring-out life's age.

Though aloft on turf or perch or poor low stage
   Both sing sometimes the sweetest, sweetest spells,
   Yet both droop deadly sometimes in their cells
Or wring their barriers in bursts of fear or rage.

Not that the sweet-fowl, song-fowl, needs no rest —
Why, hear him, hear him babble & drop down to his nest,
   But his own nest, wild nest, no prison.

Man's spirit will be flesh-bound, when found at best,
But uncumbered: meadow-down is not distressed
   For a rainbow footing it nor he for his bones risen.

Emma Lazarus (1849–1887) was a successful Jewish-American author and poet. She advocated for Jewish refugees who had fled Russia to escape the pogroms, and she helped establish the Hebrew Technical Institute to offer Jews vocational training so that they could become self-supporting. Emma Lazarus wrote "The New Colossus" for an auction to raise funds to build the pedestal for the Statue of Liberty. Her poem was eventually cast onto a bronze plaque and mounted on the pedestal.

In your introduction, you might tell the students about the Colossus of Rhodes, "the brazen giant of Greek fame," referred to in this poem. Students might be told a bit about the origin of the statue—that it was a gift from the French to recognize America as a champion of liberty and to commemorate the alliance between the two nations. In conversation with the students, you could explore the themes of immigration, asylum, and the quest for freedom.

The New Colossus (1903)
Emma Lazarus

Not like the brazen giant of Greek fame,
With conquering limbs astride from land to land;
Here at our sea-washed, sunset gates shall stand
A mighty woman with a torch, whose flame
Is the imprisoned lightning, and her name
Mother of Exiles. From her beacon-hand
Glows world-wide welcome; her mild eyes command
The air-bridged harbor that twin cities frame.
"Keep, ancient lands, your storied pomp!" cries she
With silent lips. "Give me your tired, your poor,
Your huddled masses yearning to breathe free,
The wretched refuse of your teeming shore.
Send these, the homeless, tempest-tost to me,
I lift my lamp beside the golden door!"

As eighth graders mature, they become more aware of the complexities of human relationships and begin to appreciate literature that illuminates these complexities. In your introduction, you might refer to the relationships between European nations and how these relationships were changing at the beginning of the 20th century. You might also have the students consider the subject of boundaries between people and nations, and why they are necessary.

Robert Frost (1874–1963) was one of the best-known poets of his time. His poems often depicted scenes from rural life in New England that seem simple but pose deep philosophical and moral questions.

Mending Wall (1914)
Robert Frost

Something there is that doesn't love a wall,
That sends the frozen-ground-swell under it,
And spills the upper boulders in the sun;
And makes gaps even two can pass abreast.
The work of hunters is another thing:
I have come after them and made repair
Where they have left not one stone on a stone,
But they would have the rabbit out of hiding,
To please the yelping dogs. The gaps I mean,
No one has seen them made or heard them made,
But at spring mending-time we find them there.
I let my neighbor know beyond the hill;
And on a day we meet to walk the line
And set the wall between us once again.

We keep the wall between us as we go.
To each the boulders that have fallen to each.
And some are loaves and some so nearly balls
We have to use a spell to make them balance:
'Stay where you are until our backs are turned!'
We wear our fingers rough with handling them.
Oh, just another kind of out-door game,
One on a side. It comes to little more:
There where it is we do not need the wall:
He is all pine and I am apple orchard.
My apple trees will never get across
And eat the cones under his pines, I tell him.
He only says, 'Good fences make good neighbors.'
Spring is the mischief in me, and I wonder
If I could put a notion in his head:
'*Why* do they make good neighbors? Isn't it
Where there are cows? But here there are no cows.
Before I built a wall I'd ask to know
What I was walling in or walling out,
And to whom I was like to give offense.
Something there is that doesn't love a wall,
That wants it down.' I could say 'Elves' to him,
But it's not elves exactly, and I'd rather
He said it for himself. I see him there
Bringing a stone grasped firmly by the top
In each hand, like an old-stone savage armed.
He moves in darkness as it seems to me,
Not of woods only and the shade of trees.
He will not go behind his father's saying,
And he likes having thought of it so well
He says again, 'Good fences make good neighbors.'

Wilfred Owen (1893–1918) was one of the leading poets of the World War I. He enlisted in the British army at the age of 20 and endured the horrors of trench warfare. Owen was hospitalized for shell shock, and while he was recuperating, he met a fellow poet, Siegfried Sassoon, who inspired him to write about his wartime experiences. Owen returned to active duty in July of 1918 and was killed one week before the signing of the Armistice.

If you have presented scenes from World War I, you may not need to elaborate on the situations in this poem. Your introduction might include the translation of Latin phrase by Horace: "It is sweet and fitting to die for one's country,"* and you may wish to have the students respond to this idea both before and after they hear the poem.

Dulce et Decorum Est (1920)
Wilfred Owen

Bent double, like old beggars under sacks,
Knock-kneed, coughing like hags, we cursed through sludge,
Till on the haunting flares we turned our backs,
And towards our distant rest began to trudge.
Men marched asleep. Many had lost their boots,
But limped on, blood-shod. All went lame; all blind;
Drunk with fatigue; deaf even to the hoots
Of gas-shells dropping softly behind.

Gas! GAS! Quick, boys!—An ecstasy of fumbling
Fitting the clumsy helmets just in time,
But someone still was yelling out and stumbling
And flound'ring like a man in fire or lime.—
Dim through the misty panes and thick green light,
As under a green sea, I saw him drowning.

In all my dreams before my helpless sight,
He plunges at me, guttering, choking, drowning.

If in some smothering dreams, you too could pace
Behind the wagon that we flung him in,
And watch the white eyes writhing in his face,
His hanging face, like a devil's sick of sin;
If you could hear, at every jolt, the blood
Come gargling from the froth-corrupted lungs,
Obscene as cancer, bitter as the cud
Of vile, incurable sores on innocent tongues,—
My friend, you would not tell with such high zest
To children ardent for some desperate glory,
The old Lie: *Dulce et decorum est pro patria mori.*

Lieutenant-Colonel John McCrae (1872–1918) was a Canadian author and physician who is best known for his war-memorial poem "In Flanders Fields." McCrae wrote this poem the day after one of his closest friends was buried in a cemetery where poppies bloomed. After serving as a medical officer for over three years, McCrae died of pneumonia in early 1918.

If you have presented scenes from World War I, you do not need to describe the scene of the poem, but your introduction might consider the poet's device of having the dead speak, and you might discuss the theme of this poem along with the poems by Wilfred Owen and Siegfried Sassoon.

In Flanders Fields (1915)
John McCrae

In Flanders fields the poppies blow
Between the crosses, row on row,
    That mark our place; and in the sky
    The larks, still bravely singing, fly
Scarce heard amid the guns below.

We are the Dead. Short days ago
We lived, felt dawn, saw sunset glow,
    Loved and were loved, and now we lie,
        In Flanders fields.

Take up our quarrel with the foe:
To you from failing hands we throw
    The torch; be yours to hold it high.
    If ye break faith with us who die
We shall not sleep, though poppies grow
        In Flanders fields.

Reconciliation (1918)
Siegfried Sassoon

When you are standing at your hero's grave,
Or near some homeless village where he died,
Remember, through your heart's rekindling pride,
The German soldiers who were loyal and brave.
Men fought like brutes; and hideous things were done,
And you have nourished hatred harsh and blind.
But in that Golgotha perhaps you'll find
The mothers of the men who killed your son.

The Poet as Hero (1916)
Siegfried Sassoon

You've heard me, scornful, harsh, and discontented,
    Mocking and loathing War: you've asked me why
Of my old, silly sweetness I've repented—
    My ecstasies changed to an ugly cry.
You are aware that once I sought the Grail,
    Riding in armour bright, serene and strong;
And it was told that through my infant wail
    There rose immortal semblances of song.
But now I've said good-bye to Galahad,
    And am no more the knight of dreams and show:
For lust and senseless hatred make me glad,
    And my killed friends are with me where I go.
Wound for red wound I burn to smite their wrongs;
And there is absolution in my songs.

Claude McKay (1890–1948) was a Jamaican-American writer and poet who depicted the many challenges that Black Americans face: racism, segregation, discrimination, and economic suppression. Your introduction to these poems should provide enough context for your students to appreciate the power of his work.

If We Must Die
Claude McKay

If we must die, let it not be like hogs
Hunted and penned in an inglorious spot,
While round us bark the mad and hungry dogs,
Making their mock at our accursèd lot.
If we must die, O let us nobly die,
So that our precious blood may not be shed
In vain; then even the monsters we defy
Shall be constrained to honor us though dead!
O kinsmen! we must meet the common foe!
Though far outnumbered let us show us brave,
And for their thousand blows deal one death-blow!
What though before us lies the open grave?
Like men we'll face the murderous, cowardly pack,
Pressed to the wall, dying, but fighting back!

America (1921)
Claude McKay

Although she feeds me bread of bitterness,
And sinks into my throat her tiger's tooth,
Stealing my breath of life, I will confess
I love this cultured hell that tests my youth.
Her vigor flows like tides into my blood,
Giving me strength erect against her hate,
Her bigness sweeps my being like a flood.
Yet, as a rebel fronts a king in state,
I stand within her walls with not a shred
Of terror, malice, not a word of jeer.
Darkly I gaze into the days ahead,
And see her might and granite wonders there,
Beneath the touch of Time's unerring hand,
Like priceless treasures sinking in the sand.

James Mercer Langston Hughes (1901–1967) was an American poet, social activist, novelist, and playwright. One of the first innovators of jazz poetry, Hughes became one of the leaders of the Harlem Renaissance. In your introduction, you might present the idea that the poem's brevity makes it especially powerful.

Minstrel Man (1925)
Langston Hughes

Because my mouth
Is wide with laughter
And my throat
Is deep with song,
You do not think
I suffer after
I have held my pain
So long.
Because my mouth
Is wide with laughter,
You do not hear
My inner cry,
Because my feet
Are gay with dancing,
You do not know
I die.

Eighth graders are interested in all aspects of the human experience, including death. "Immortality" will appeal to them because it makes its point so directly and through such vivid images. This poem was mistakenly attributed to Mary Elizabeth Frye, who distributed the poem under her name, but it was written by Clare Harner (1909–1977), who wrote it shortly after the death of her brother and who published it in 1934 in a poetry magazine. Your introduction might include a conversation about death, bereavement, and—if you think it appropriate—reincarnation.

Immortality (1934)
Clare Harner

> Do not stand
>   By my grave, and weep.
> I am not there,
>   I do not sleep—
> I am the thousand winds that blow
> I am the diamond glints in snow
> I am the sunlight on ripened grain,
> I am the gentle, autumn rain.
> As you awake with morning's hush,
> I am the swift, up-flinging rush
> Of quiet birds in circling flight,
> I am the day transcending night.
>   Do not stand
>   By my grave, and cry—
>   I am not there,
>   I did not die.

Margaret Walker (1915–1998) was one of the leading African-American writers of the mid-20th century, whose writing called for racial awakening. Your introduction might help orient your students to the less-familiar references. Whether it is read or recited, the poem can be divided among groups or individual students, who can individualize each stanza's message.

For My People (1937)
Margaret Walker

> For my people everywhere singing their slave songs
>   repeatedly: their dirges and their ditties and their blues
>   and jubilees, praying their prayers nightly to an
>   unknown god, bending their knees humbly to an
>   unseen power;
>
> For my people lending their strength to the years, to the
>   gone years and the now years and the maybe years,
>   washing ironing cooking scrubbing sewing mending
>   hoeing plowing digging planting pruning patching
>   dragging along never gaining never reaping never
>   knowing and never understanding;

For my playmates in the clay and dust and sand of Alabama
   backyards playing baptizing and preaching and doctor
   and jail and soldier and school and mama and cooking
   and playhouse and concert and store and hair and
   Miss Choomby and company;

For the cramped bewildered years we went to school to learn
   to know the reasons why and the answers to and the
   people who and the places where and the days when, in
   memory of the bitter hours when we discovered we
   were black and poor and small and different and nobody
   cared and nobody wondered and nobody understood;

For the boys and girls who grew in spite of these things to
   be man and woman, to laugh and dance and sing and
   play and drink their wine and religion and success, to
   marry their playmates and bear children and then die
   of consumption and anemia and lynching;

For my people thronging 47th Street in Chicago and Lenox
   Avenue in New York and Rampart Street in New
   Orleans, lost disinherited dispossessed and happy
   people filling the cabarets and taverns and other
   people's pockets and needing bread and shoes and milk and
   land and money and something—something all our own;

For my people walking blindly spreading joy, losing time
   being lazy, sleeping when hungry, shouting when
   burdened, drinking when hopeless, tied, and shackled
   and tangled among ourselves by the unseen creatures
   who tower over us omnisciently and laugh;

For my people blundering and groping and floundering in
   the dark of churches and schools and clubs
   and societies, associations and councils and committees and
   conventions, distressed and disturbed and deceived and
   devoured by money-hungry glory-craving leeches,
   preyed on by facile force of state and fad and novelty, by
   false prophet and holy believer;

For my people standing staring trying to fashion a better way
   from confusion, from hypocrisy and misunderstanding,
   trying to fashion a world that will hold all the people,
   all the faces, all the adams and eves and their countless generations;

> Let a new earth rise. Let another world be born. Let a
>   bloody peace be written in the sky. Let a second
>   generation full of courage issue forth; let a people
>   loving freedom come to growth. Let a beauty full of
>   healing and a strength of final clenching be the pulsing
>   in our spirits and our blood. Let the martial songs
>   be written, let the dirges disappear. Let a race of men now
>   rise and take control.

There are many other speeches and quotes from American History that can be read or recited, but Martin Luther King Jr.'s "I Have a Dream" speech is especially worth learning. I recommend watching a video of the speech to create a context. Because it is so long, I suggest that students recite only the latter portion of the speech. Students can choose the section that they find particularly meaningful, and they can recite the speech in sequence ending in unison with the rousing words:

"I Have a Dream" Speech (1963) (excerpt)

> When we let freedom ring, when we let it ring from every tenement and every hamlet, from every state and every city, we will be able to speed up that day when all of God's children, black men and white men, Jews and Gentiles, Protestants and Catholics, will be able to join hands and sing in the words of the old spiritual, "Free at last, free at last. Thank God Almighty, we are free at last."

The following quote may appeal to your students because it places individuals at the center of their world of relationships. Haim Ginott (1922–1973) was a child psychologist and parent educator who pioneered techniques for talking with children.

The Decisive Element (1972)
Haim G. Ginott

> I have come to the frightening conclusion that I am the decisive element.
> It is my personal approach that creates the climate.
> It is my daily mood that makes the weather.
> I possess tremendous power to make a life miserable or joyous.
> I can be a tool of torture, or an instrument of inspiration.
> I can humiliate or humor, hurt or heal.
> In all situations, it is my response that decides whether a crisis will be escalated
>   or de-escalated, and a person humanized or dehumanized.
> If we treat people as they are, we make them worse.
> If we treat people as they ought to be, we help them become what they are
>   capable of becoming.

Maya Angelou (1928–2014) was a prolific American writer and poet. The first of her seven autobiographies, *I Know Why the Caged Bird Sings*, brought her international acclaim. Maya Angelou worked in the civil rights movement with Dr. Martin Luther King Jr. and Malcolm X. Her poem "Caged Bird" can be found in the seventh-grade section, but it can be learned in eighth grade because it presents such a powerful contrast between freedom and enslavement. "Still I Rise" and "Life Doesn't Frighten Me" both express Maya Angelou's strength and defiance.

Still I Rise (1978)
Maya Angelou

You may write me down in history
With your bitter, twisted lies,
You may trod me in the very dirt
But still, like dust, I'll rise.

Does my sassiness upset you?
Why are you beset with gloom?
'Cause I walk like I've got oil wells
Pumping in my living room.

Just like moons and like suns,
With the certainty of tides,
Just like hopes springing high,
Still I'll rise.

Did you want to see me broken?
Bowed head and lowered eyes?
Shoulders falling down like teardrops,
Weakened by my soulful cries?

Does my haughtiness offend you?
Don't you take it awful hard
'Cause I laugh like I've got gold mines
Diggin' in my own backyard.

You may shoot me with your words,
You may cut me with your eyes,
You may kill me with your hatefulness,
But still, like air, I'll rise.

Does my sexiness upset you?
Does it come as a surprise
That I dance like I've got diamonds
At the meeting of my thighs?

Out of the huts of history's shame
I rise
Up from a past that's rooted in pain
I rise
I'm a black ocean, leaping and wide,
Welling and swelling I bear in the tide.

Leaving behind nights of terror and fear
I rise
Into a daybreak that's wondrously clear
I rise
Bringing the gifts that my ancestors gave,
I am the dream and the hope of the slave.
I rise
I rise
I rise.

Life Doesn't Frighten Me (1993)
Maya Angelou

Shadows on the wall
Noises down the hall
Life doesn't frighten me at all

Bad dogs barking loud
Big ghosts in a cloud
Life doesn't frighten me at all

Mean old Mother Goose
Lions on the loose
They don't frighten me at all

Dragons breathing flame
On my counterpane
That doesn't frighten me at all.
I go boo
Make them shoo
I make fun
Way they run
I won't cry
So they fly
I just smile
They go wild

Life doesn't frighten me at all.

Tough guys fight
All alone at night
Life doesn't frighten me at all.

Panthers in the park
Strangers in the dark
No, they don't frighten me at all.

That new classroom where
Boys all pull my hair
(Kissy little girls
With their hair in curls)
They don't frighten me at all.

Don't show me frogs and snakes
And listen for my scream,
If I'm afraid at all
It's only in my dreams.

I've got a magic charm
That I keep up my sleeve
I can walk the ocean floor
And never have to breathe.

Life doesn't frighten me at all
Not at all
Not at all.

Life doesn't frighten me at all.

Maria Wislawa Anna Szymborska (1923–2012) was a Polish poet and essayist, who won international recognition when she was awarded the Nobel Prize in Literature in 1996. In your introduction, you might discuss some of the many the mundane effects of war, and you might ask your students to think about the many "someones" who have to "clean up."

The End and the Beginning (1993)
Wislawa Szymborska

After every war
someone has to clean up.
Things won't
straighten themselves up, after all.
Someone has to push the rubble
to the side of the road,
so the corpse-filled wagons
can pass.

Someone has to get mired
in scum and ashes,
sofa springs,
splintered glass,
and bloody rags.
Someone has to drag in a girder
to prop up a wall,
Someone has to glaze a window,
rehang a door.
Photogenic it's not,
and takes years.
All the cameras have left
for another war.
We'll need the bridges back,
and new railway stations.
Sleeves will go ragged
from rolling them up.
Someone, broom in hand,
still recalls the way it was.
Someone else listens
and nods with unsevered head.
But already there are those nearby
starting to mill about
who will find it dull.
From out of the bushes
sometimes someone still unearths
rusted-out arguments
and carries them to the garbage pile.
Those who knew
what was going on here
must make way
for those who know little.
And less than little.
And finally as little as nothing.
In the grass that has overgrown
causes and effects,
someone must be stretched out
blade of grass in his mouth
gazing at the clouds.

William Carlos Williams (1883–1963) was an American writer and poet who worked as a physician for over forty years. Williams invented a uniquely American form of poetry which focused on the everyday circumstances of life. He saw poetry as akin to painting, where images can be brought to life. In your introduction to this poem, you might speak about the theme of old age and familiarize your students with the images Williams presents. Once they have begun learning the poem, see if they find a correlation between the images, the theme, and the title.

To Waken an Old Lady (2013)
William Carlos Williams

Old age is
a flight of small
cheeping birds
skimming
bare trees
above a snow glaze.
Gaining and failing
they are buffeted
by a dark wind —
But what?
On harsh weedstalks
the flock has rested —
the snow
is covered with broken
seed husks
and the wind tempered
with a shrill
piping of plenty.

Amanda Gorman (1982–) is a contemporary American poet whose work focuses on oppression, feminism, and race. She spoke "The Hill We Climb" at President Joe Biden's inauguration in 2021. In your introduction you might include some details of her biography, and as you work on the poem, students might discuss its themes in light of their own experiences. This poem is probably too long to memorize, so you can have your students read it or divide it into sections for recitation.

The Hill We Climb (2021)
Amanda Gorman

When day comes we ask ourselves,
where can we find light in this never-ending shade?
The loss we carry,
a sea we must wade
We've braved the belly of the beast.
We've learned that quiet isn't always peace,

and the norms and notions
of what just is
isn't always just-ice.
And yet the dawn is ours
before we knew it,
somehow we do it.
Somehow we've weathered and witnessed
a nation that isn't broken
but simply unfinished.
We, the successors of a country and a time
where a skinny Black girl
descended from slaves and raised by a single mother
can dream of becoming president
only to find herself reciting for one.
And yes, we are far from polished,
far from pristine,
but that doesn't mean we are
striving to form a union that is perfect.
We are striving to forge a union with purpose,
to compose a country committed to all cultures, colors, characters, and
conditions of man.
And so we lift our gazes not to what stands between us
but what stands before us.
We close the divide because we know, to put our future first,
we must first put our differences aside.
We lay down our arms
so we can reach out our arms
to one another.
We seek harm to none and harmony for all.
Let the globe, if nothing else, say this is true:
That even as we grieved, we grew;
that even as we hurt, we hoped;
that even as we tired, we tried;
that we'll forever be tied together, victorious,
not because we will never again know defeat
but because we will never again sow division.
Scripture tells us to envision
that everyone shall sit under their own vine and fig tree
and no one shall make them afraid.
If we're to live up to our own time
then victory won't lie in the blade
but in all the bridges we've made.
That is the promise to glade,
the hill we climb
if only we dare it,

because being American is more than a pride we inherit—
it's the past we step into
and how we repair it.
We've seen a force that would shatter our nation
rather than share it
would destroy our country if it meant delaying democracy.
And this effort very nearly succeeded.
But while democracy can be periodically delayed,
it can never be permanently defeated.
In this truth,
in this faith we trust,
for while we have our eyes on the future,
history has its eyes on us.
This is the era of just redemption
we feared at its inception.
We did not feel prepared to be the heirs
of such a terrifying hour
but within it we found the power
to author a new chapter,
to offer hope and laughter to ourselves.
So while once we asked,
how could we possibly prevail over catastrophe,
now we assert,
how could catastrophe possibly prevail over us?
We will not march back to what was
but move to what shall be:
a country that is bruised but whole,
benevolent but bold,
fierce, and free.
We will not be turned around
or interrupted by intimidation
because we know our inaction and inertia
will be the inheritance of the next generation.
Our blunders become their burdens.
But one thing is certain:
If we merge mercy with might,
and might with right,
then love becomes our legacy
and change our children's birthright.
So let us leave behind a country
better than the one we were left with.
Every breath from my bronze-pounded chest,
we will raise this wounded world into a wondrous one.
We will rise from the gold-limned hills of the west,
we will rise from the windswept northeast

where our forefathers first realized revolution,
we will rise from the lake-rimmed cities of the midwestern states,
we will rise from the sunbaked south.
We will rebuild, reconcile, and recover
in every known nook of our nation and
every corner called our country,
our people diverse and beautiful will emerge,
battered and beautiful.
When day comes we step out of the shade,
aflame and unafraid.
The new dawn blooms as we free it.
For there is always light,
if only we're brave enough to see it,
if only we're brave enough to be it.

SPEECH EXERCISES

Geographical Fugue
Ernst Toch

In earlier grades, students worked on tongue twisters, speech rounds, quodlibets and polyphonic speech pieces. In eighth grade the speech work can come to a culmination by performing Ernst Toch's "Geographical Fugue"—a complex spoken-word piece for four voices. Working on this will require students to read rhythmic notation and to hold their own in the context of the other parts. If you are not familiar with it, I encourage you to find it online and determine whether your students could do it.

Radio Announcer's Tests

Radio announcer's tests were developed in the 1920s to see whether prospective announcers had the necessary speaking skills to be hired. Announcer's tests assessed memory, repetition, enunciation, diction, and breath control. Here is a famous example:

Penelope Cholmondely

Penelope Cholmondely raised her azure eyes from the crabbed scenario. She meandered among the congeries of her memoirs. There was the Kinetic Algernon, a choleric artificer of icons and triptychs, who wanted to write a trilogy. For years she had stifled her risibilities with dour moods. His asthma caused him to sough like the zephyrs among the tamarack.

This announcer's test that was created in the 1940s and popularized on stage, radio, and television by Jerry Lewis (1926–2017), an American comedian, actor, and filmmaker who raised vast sums of money for research into muscular dystrophy.

To learn the test, each line can be spoken separately and then repeated by the students until they have completed the whole series.

To use this exercise for breath control, students can try to recite each line in one breath.

After the students have learned it, you can challenge them to use this model to compose their own versions.

One Hen, Two Ducks

One hen

One hen; Two ducks

One hen; Two ducks; Three squawking geese
One hen; Two ducks; Three squawking geese; Four limerick oysters

One hen; Two ducks; Three squawking geese; Four limerick oysters; Five corpulent porpoises

One hen; Two ducks; Three squawking geese; Four limerick oysters; Five corpulent porpoises; Six pairs of Don Alverzo's tweezers

One hen; Two ducks; Three squawking geese; Four limerick oysters; Five corpulent porpoises; Six pairs of Don Alverzo's tweezers; Seven thousand Macedonians in full battle array

One hen; Two ducks; Three squawking geese; Four limerick oysters; Five corpulent porpoises; Six pairs of Don Alverzo's tweezers; Seven thousand Macedonians in full battle array; Eight brass monkeys from the ancient sacred crypts of Egypt

One hen; Two ducks; Three squawking geese; Four limerick oysters; Five corpulent porpoises; Six pairs of Don Alverzo's tweezers; Seven thousand Macedonians in full battle array; Eight brass monkeys from the ancient sacred crypts of Egypt; Nine apathetic, sympathetic, diabetic old men on roller skates, with a marked propensity toward procrastination and sloth

One hen; Two ducks; Three squawking geese; Four limerick oysters; Five corpulent porpoises; Six pairs of Don Alverzo's tweezers; Seven thousand Macedonians in full battle array; Eight brass monkeys from the ancient sacred crypts of Egypt; Nine apathetic, sympathetic, diabetic old men on roller skates, with a marked propensity toward procrastination and sloth; Ten lyrical, spherical, diabolical denizens of the deep who all stall around the corner of the quo of the quay of the quivery, all at the same time.

Patter Songs

Eighth graders enjoy recitations that challenge their articulation and breath control. Patter songs (which can be spoken instead of sung) from musicals and operettas are challenging and fun. If you are not familiar with patter songs, I encourage you to look up: "I am the Very Model of a Modern Major General" from *The Pirates of Penzance*; "My Eyes Are Fully Open to My Awful Situation," from *Ruddigore*; "The Train Song" and "Ya Got Trouble" from *The Music Man*; and "The Museum Song" from *Barnum*. The lyrics and lists of other patter songs can be found online.

Patter Poetry

"Errantry," by J.R.R. Tolkien challenges students to speak clearly and quickly. Because it is so long, it may be better to read—rather than memorize—the poem, or to have different students memorize sections and to piece the entire poem together from the individual contributions.

J.R.R. Tolkien (1892–1973) was a professor at Oxford University who became well-known as the author of *The Hobbit* and *The Lord of the Rings*. In your introduction to this poem, you might introduce the students to some of the unusual words in the poem, or you can read it first and then see if they can figure out the words' meanings.

Errantry
J.R.R. Tolkien

There was a merry passenger,
a messenger a mariner:
he built a gilded gondola
to wander in and had in her
a load of yellow oranges
and porridge for his provender;
he perfumed her with marjoram,
and cardamom and lavender.

He called the winds of Argosies,
with cargoes in to carry him,
across the rivers seventeen,
that lay between to tarry him.
He landed all in loneliness,
where stonily the pebbles on
the running river Derrilyn,
goes merrily for ever on.
He journeyed then through meadow-lands,
to shadow-land that dreary lay,
and under hill and over hill,
went roving still a weary way.

He sat and sang a melody,
his errantry a tarrying,
he begged a pretty butterfly,
that fluttered by to marry him.
She scorned him and she scoffed at him,
she laughed at him unpitying,
so long he studied wizardry,
and sigaldry and smithying.

He wove a tissue airy thin,
to snare her in; to follow her,
he made him beetle-leatherwing,
and feather wing of swallow hair.

He caught her in bewilderment,
with filament of spider-thread.
He made her soft pavilions,
of lilies and a bridal bed,
of flowers and of thistle-down,
to nestle down and rest her in,
and silken webs of filmy white,
and silver light he dressed her in.

He threaded gems and necklaces,
but recklessly she squandered them,
and fell to bitter quarrelling,
then sorrowing he wandered on,
and there he left her withering
as shivering he fled away;
with windy weather following,
on swallow-wing he sped away.

He passed the achipelagoes,
where yellow grows the marigold,
with countless silver fountains are,
and mountains are of fairy-gold.
He took to war and foraying,
a-harrying beyond the sea,
and roaming over Belmary,
and Thellamie and Fantasie.

He made a shield and morion,
of coral and of ivory.
A sword he made of emerald,
and terrible his rivalry,
with elven knights of Aerie

and Faerie, with paladins
that golden-haired, and shining-eyed
came riding by, and challenged him.

Of crystal was his habergeon,
his scabbard of chalcedony,
with silver tipped and plenilune,
his spear was hewn of ebony.
His javelins were of malachite
and stalactite—he brandished them,
and went and fought the dragon flies,
of Paradise, and vanquished them.

He battled with the Dumbledors,
the Hummerhorns, and Honeybees,
and won the Golden Honeycomb,
and running home on sunny seas,
in ship of leaves and gossamer,
with blossom for a canopy,
he sat and sang, and furbished up,
and burnished up his panoply.

He tarried for a little while,
in little isles that lonely lay,
and found their naught but blowing grass.
And so at last, the only way he took, and turned,
and coming home with honeycomb,
to memory his message came,
and errand too!
In derring-do and glamoury,
he had forgot them,
journeying and tourneying, a wanderer.

So now he must depart again,
and start again his gondola,
for ever still a messenger
a passenger, a tarrier,
a roving as a feather does,
a weather-driven mariner.

TONGUE TWISTERS

Tongue twisters can be used in eighth grade as warm-up exercises to prepare for recitation or to bring a measure of levity into the morning, when students may feel tired and not yet fully present.

Tongue twisters can easily 'grow old' in eighth grade, so it is important to not to overwork them—a week is probably the limit. During that week, you can work on three or four tongue twisters, exchanging them for new ones when students have become adept. One way to keep tongue twisters 'fresh' is to aim for immediate recall; another is to create quodlibets where lines from one tongue twister alternate with the lines from another.

Several variations of the Woodchuck verse are provided in the seventh grade chapter. I encourage you to challenge your students to come up with others. Here is one example:

> How many snacks could a snack stacker stack,
> If a snack stacker could stack snacks?
> She would stack as many snacks
> As the snacks could be stacked
> If a snack stacker could stack snacks.

Here are some more tongue twisters that your students may enjoy. Additional examples may be found at the end of the chapters for Grades 5, 6, and 7.

> Lesser leather never weathered wetter weather better.
> Wetter weather never weathered lesser leather less.

> Seven sleazy shysters in sharkskin suits sold sheared sealskins to seasick sailors.

> There was a minimum of cinnamon in the aluminum pan.

> Aluminum linoleum. Aluminum linoleum. Aluminum linoleum.
> Aluminum linoleum. Linoleum aluminum.

> Don't pamper damp scamp tramps that camp under ramp lamps.

> Girl gargoyle, guy gargoyle. Girl gargoyle, guy gargoyle. Girl gargoyle, guy gargoyle.

> Sarah sitting in her Chevrolet,
> All she does is sits and shifts,
> All she does is sits and shifts.

These next three verses work well as rounds.

The Liquor Stock

If you stick a stock of liquor in your locker,
It's slick to stick a lock upon your stock,
Or some stickler who is slicker
Will stick you of your liquor
If you fail to lock your liquor
With a lock!

To Sit in Solemn Silence
W.S. Gilbert

To sit in solemn silence in a dull, dark dock,
In a pestilential prison, with a life-long lock,
Awaiting the sensation of a short, sharp shock,
From a cheap and chippy chopper on a big black block!
A dull, dark dock, a life-long lock,
A short, sharp shock, a big black block!

Sad, Glad, Mad

Oh, the sadness of her sadness when she's sad.
Oh, the gladness of her gladness when she's glad.
But the sadness of her sadness and the gladness of her gladness
Are nothing like her madness when she's mad.

Bank Books

Please bring the black-backed blank bank book back.
If you can't bring the black-backed blank bank book back,
Then bring the blue-backed blank bank book back.

Gertie's grandma grew aghast at Gertie's grammar.
Gertie's grammar made her grandma grow aghast.

The old school scold sold the school coal scuttle.

Twixt six thick thumbs stick six thick sticks.

Ike ships ice chips in ice chip ships.
The chips he ships are ice chips, I'm sure.

Shirley Simms shrewdly shuns sunshine and sleet.

The bleak breeze blights the brightly blooming blossom.

If silly Sally will shilly shally
Shall silly Willy willy nilly shilly shally too?

This is the catastrophic hypothesis of the suppositious apothecary.

Top chopstick shops stock top chopsticks.
While cheap chop suey shops stock cheap soup chips.

For French shrimp try a French shrimp shop;
For fresh fish try Fred's fish fry.

Real weird rear wheels.

If you notice this notice, you will notice that this notice is not worth noticing.

Does your sport shop stock short socks with spots?

They have left the thrift shop, and lost both their theatre tickets and the volume of valuable licenses and coupons for free theatrical frills and thrills.

Pick a partner and practice passing,
For if you pass proficiently,
Perhaps you'll play professionally.

"Whodunit?" uses the same technique as the famous comedy routine by Abbott and Costello, "Who's on First?" that students will enjoy seeing on video.

Whodunit?

This is a story about four people named Everybody, Somebody, Anybody, and Nobody.
There was an important job to be done and Everybody was sure that Somebody would do it.
Anybody could have done it, but Nobody did it.
Somebody got angry about that, because it was Everybody's job.
Everybody thought Anybody could do it, but Nobody realized that Everybody wouldn't do it.
It ended up that Everybody blamed Somebody when Nobody did what Anybody could have done.

References

Blishen, Edward (compiler). *Oxford Book of Poetry for Children.* London: Oxford University Press. 1963.

Ferris, Helen. *Favorite Poems Old and New.* (1957). Random House.

Jaffke, Christoph. *Rhythms, Rhymes, Games and Songs for the Lower School.* (1992). Private Printing.

_____. *Collected Poems for Class Teachers and Eurythmists.* (1986). Private Printing.

Jaffke, Christoph and Magda Maier. (1986). *Poems for the Middle and Upper School.* Private Printing.

_____. *Tongue Twisters and Speech Exercises.* (1983). Private Printing.

Karshner, Roger. *You Said a Mouthful: Tongue Twisters to Tangle, Titillate, Test and Tease.* (1993). Dramaline Publications.

Kennedy, David. *The Waldorf Book of Poetry.* (2012). Living Arts Books.

_____. *The Waldorf Book of Animal Poetry.* (2013). Living Arts Books.

Parkin, Ken. *Anthology of British Tongue Twisters.* (2015). Samuel French.

Seachrist, Elizabeth Hough. *One Thousand Poems for Children.* (1946). Macrae-Smith.

Thomas, Heather. *A Journey through Time in Verse and Rhyme.* (1987) Floris Books.

Rosenbloom, Joseph. *World's Toughest Tongue Twisters.* (1986). Sterling Publishing Co.

_____. *Twist These on Your Tongue.* (1978). Thomas Nelson.

Schwartz, Alvin. *A Twister of Twists, A Tangler of Tongues.* (1972). Harper & Row.

Index by Title

23rd Psalm, 114

A Cautionary Tale, 59
A Hop to Tahiti, 68
A Jelly-Fish, 26
A Proper Cup of Coffee, 101
A Tragic Story, 30
A Twister of Twists, 67
A Visit from St. Nicholas, 121
A Wet Sheet and a Flowing Sea, 80
After the Party, 31
America, 136
Annabel Lee, 89
Ant, Bee and Butterfly, 25
Antigone (excerpt), 84
At the Ringing of the Bells, 11, 44, 79, 113
Autumn, 21

Bank Books, 153
Be Strong! 52
Bitter Biting Bitterns, 67
Blazing in Gold, Quenching in Purple, 54
Bleeding Beetles, 67
Bug Blood, 36

Caged Bird, 91
Casey at the Bat, 63
Cheap Sea Trips, 35
Chuckling Chickens, 34
Columbus, 81
Concord Hymn, 124

Daffodils, 56
Desiderata, 20
Dulce et Decorum Est, 133
Dusting the Bust, 68

English, 28
Errantry, 149
Evangeline: A Tale of Acadie (Prelude), 20

Fat Cats, Red Hats, 66
For My People, 137
From Ancient Persia, 12

Gathas of Zarathustra (excerpt), 13
Geographical Fugue, 147
Gettysburg Address, 127
Glue Gun Glue, 35

Hannibal, 46
He Walketh by Day, 14
Hercules, 17
Hewer Hugh, 35, 68
How much wood would a woodchuck chuck, 104
Hymn in Praise of Ra, 15
Hymn of Creation, 12
Hymn to Prometheus, 18
Hymn to the Sun, 15

I Dug and Dug amongst the Snow, 24
"I Have a Dream" Speech (excerpt), 139
If I Can Stop One Heart From Breaking, 88
If We Must Die, 125
Immortality, 137
Indian Names, 122
In Flanders Fields, 134
Invictus, 129
Isaac Newton Quote, 83

Jabberwocky, 29

Lake Isle of Innisfree, 86
Letter to the Corinthians (excerpt), 114

Life Doesn't Frighten Me, 57, 141
Lines Composed in a Wood on a Windy Day, 87
Lines from Invocation of Peace, 19
Lord Ullin's Daughter, 93

May Wisdom Shine through Me, 11, 44, 78, 113
Meditation, 118
Mending Wall, 131
Minstrel Man, 136
Mutter Shutter, 68

Need a Needle? 66
Nicholas Copernicus Quote, 83

O Captain, My Captain, 128
O Roma Nobilis, 45
Ode to Zeus, 17
Ode: Intimations of Immortality, 84
Olympic Oath, 17
One Hen, Two Ducks, 148
Opening Lines of *The Aeneid*, 45, 46
Opening Lines of *The Iliad*, 16
Ozymandias of Egypt, 53

Patter Songs, 149
Penelope Cholmondely, 147
Pirate Booty, 68
Pop's Bottles, 35
Preamble to the Constitution, 119
Prometheus Bound (excerpt), 19

Quote from Isaac Newton, 83
Quote from Nicholas Copernicus, 83

Reconciliation, 134
Rime of the Ancient Mariner (excerpt), 119
Roasting Roaches, 66

Sad, Glad, Mad, 153
Salutation to the Dawn, 52
Sam's Swimming, 38
Sea Fever, 79
Selections from Julius Caesar, 47, 48
Shame on Sam, 38
Sick, 31

Slippery Snakes, 36, 73
Song of the Camels, 55
Sonnet 18, 117
Sonnet 29, 117
Speech by Chief Seattle (excerpt), 125
Stately Verse, 32
Still I Rise, 140
Stopping by Woods on a Snowy Evening, 56
Superlatives, 103

The Aeneid, Opening Lines, 45
The Appointment in Samarra, 92
The Battle of Maldon (excerpt), 49
The Bear and the Boar, 36, 101
The Blacksmiths, 51
The Blazer Braid, 66
The Bleak Breeze Blights, 38, 69
The Blind Men and the Elephant, 99
The Caged Skylark, 130
The Canterbury Tales (excerpt from the Prologue), 50
The Charge of the Light Brigade, 125
The Decisive Element, 139
The Declaration of Independence, 118
The Destruction of Sennacherib, 95
The End and the Beginning, 142
The Epic of Gilgamesh (excerpt), 14
The Good Joan, 82
The Grip-top Sock, 102
The Highwayman, 96
The Hill We Climb, 144
The Iliad, Opening Lines, 16
The Liquor Stock, 153
The Little Metal Kettle, 102
The New Colossus, 131
The Night Light, 102
The Noble Nature, 23
The Poet as Hero, 135
The Quality of Mercy, 116
The Ride-by-Nights, 54
The Road Not Taken, 85
The Sea Wolf, 22
The Ship That Sails, 87
The Speech at the Diet of Worms (excerpt), 83
The Thief, 36, 103

The Throstle, 25
The Walrus and the Carpenter, 60
The Witch's House, 21
Theophilus Thistledown, 37, 75
There Lives in Me an Image, 11, 44, 78, 112
Think of This! 35
This England, 115
To Autumn, 88
To Every Thing There Is a Season, 115
To Sit in Solemn Silence, 153
To Thine Own Self Be True, 116
To Waken an Old Lady, 144
Tomorrow, and tomorrow, and tomorrow, 116
Tree for Two, 101
Trees, 23
Trouble, 65

Watch Out! 35
What Do We Plant, 24
Where O Where? 33
Whether the Weather, 33, 103
Who Drew What? 36
Whodunit? 154
Why English Is So Hard to Learn, 27
Willie Poems, 37

Zend Avesta (excerpt), 13

Index by First Line

A bitter biting bittern, 67
A bloke's back brake block broke, 105
A box of biscuits; a box of mixed biscuits, 40
A Chieftain, to the Highlands bound, 93
A fine field of wheat, 40, 71
A free bird leaps on the back of the wind, 91
A hunter went a-hunting, a-hunting for a hare, 71
A lump of red leather, a red leather lump, 71
A maid with a duster made a furious bluster, 68
A pessimistic pest exists amidst us, 72
A tree toad loved a she toad, 101
A truly rural frugal ruler's mural, 41
A twister of twists once twisted a twist, 67
A wet sheet and a flowing sea, 80
After every war someone has to clean up, 142
All I want is a proper cup of coffee, 101
Along the thousand roads of France, 82
Although she feeds me bread of bitterness, 136
Aluminum linoleum, 152
Amidst the mists and coldest frosts, 103
An end to words. Deeds now, 19
And now the STORM-BLAST came, 119
Arma virumque cano, Troiae qui primus ab oris, 45
Arms and the man I sing, who, forced by fate, 46
As a dare-gale skylark scanted in a dull cage, 130

Be strong! 52
Bear the sun to the earth! 12
Beautiful is Thy awakening, 15
Beautiful, babbling brooks bubble between blossoming banks, 70
Because my mouth is wide with laughter, 136
Behind him lay the gray Azores, 81
Bent double, like old beggars under sacks, 133
Better never trouble Trouble, 65
Big black bugs bleed blue black blood, 36
Blackbeard brought back black bric-a-brac, 68

Blazing in gold and quenching in purple, 54
Blows the bitter blast, 105
Borachio Mustachio Whisterifustikus, 105
By the rude bridge that arched the flood, 124
Byrhtwold maþelode, bord hafenode, 49
Byrhtwold spoke, raised his shield, 49

Can Kitty cuddle Clara's kitten? 40
Can you imagine an imaginary menagerie manager, 72
Cheek, chin, cheek, chin, cheek, chin, nose, 40
Chilly chili will become more chilly, 40
Collectible classics cause, 106
Come watch the chuckling chickens, 34
Conrad came careering round the corner, 70, 106
Crows graze in droves, 71

Dart saves dear, 106
Dashing dangerously down the dale, 40, 71, 106
Dashing Daniel defied David, 40
Deep peace, pure white of the moon to you, 19
Do not stand by my grave, and weep, 137
Does your sport shop stock short socks, 154
Don't pamper damp scamp tramps, 106, 152
Don't run along the wrong lane, 73
Double bubble gum bubbles double, 71
Drew and Lou drew drawing, 36

Fifteen frightened fluffy fowls, 40, 71
Five fashionable females flying to France, 106
For French shrimp try a French shrimp shop, 71, 154
For my people everywhere singing their slave songs, 137
Four score and seven years ago, 127
Freddy is ready to roast red roaches, 66
Friends, Romans, countrymen, lend me your ears, 48

George Gabs grabs crabs, 71, 106
Gerties grandma grew aghast at Gertie's grammar, 153
Girl gargoyle, guy gargoyle, 152
Give me the gift of a grip-top sock, 102
Go and get the glue gun glue, 35
Good, better, best, never let it rest, 103
"Goodbye, Gerty," gushed Gussie, 71

Hail to Prometheus, the Titan, 18
Hail to thee, O Ra, O perfect and eternal one, 15
Half a league, half a league, half a league onward, 125
Hard-hearted Harold hit Henry hard, 71
Have you ever watched the humble ants, 25
Hear the happy hunter's horn, 40
Heather was hoping to hop to Tahiti, 68
How can a clam cram in a clean cream can? 70
How can the red men be forgotten, 122
How many snacks could a snack stacker stack, 152
How much ground could a groundhog hog, 105
How much hair could a hair net net, 105
How much wood would a woodchuck chuck, 104

I am yesterday, today, and tomorrow, 14
I brought the blazer braid I bought, 66, 70
I can think of six thin things, 35
I cannot go to school today, 31
I could be well moved, if I were as you, 47
I do like cheap sea trips, 35
I do not know what I may appear to the world, 83
I dug and dug amongst the snow, 24
I have a new Swiss wristwatch, 35
I have come to the frightening conclusion, 139
I met a traveler from an antique land, 53
I must down to the seas again, 79
I need not your needles, 66
I need not your needles, they're needless to me, 72
I shot the city sheriff, 73, 107
I sit and slit and slit and sit, 74, 107
I take it you already know, 28

I think that I shall never see, 23
I thought a thought, 108
I wandered lonely as a cloud, 56
I will arise and go now, and go to Innisfree, 86
I would I were where I would be, 33
I'd rather be the ship that sails, 87
I'm a sheet slitter. I slit sheets, 73, 107
If fat cats all wore hats, 66
If I can stop one heart from breaking, 88
If Mary goes far out to sea, 32
If neither he sells seashells, 107
If practice makes perfect, 72, 107
If she stops at the shop where I stop, 74
If silly Sally will shilly shally, 41, 154
If we must die, let it not be like hogs, 135
If you notice this notice, 154
If you stick a stock of liquor in your locker, 153
Ike ships ice chips in ice chip ships, 40, 153
In Flanders fields the poppies blow, 134
In Huron a hewer, Hugh Hughes, 35, 68
In the family drinking well, 37
In the flaming fire we worship thee, 13
Is there a pleasant peasant present? 72
It is not growing like a tree, 23
It was many and many a year ago, 89
It was six men of Indostan, 99
It's a shame, Sam, 38
Its wicked little windows leer, 21

Jangling our jam-jars and jumping for joy, 40
Jonathan Blake ate too much cake, 31

Lesser leather never weathered wetter weather better, 106, 152
Listen to me, O Utnapishtim! 14
Look to this day! 52
Lord, make me an instrument of Thy peace, 20

Many an anemone sees an enemy anemone, 40, 71
Maud walked on the lawn, 106
May wisdom shine through me, 11, 44, 78, 113
Men munch much mush, 41, 106
Menin aeide Thea, Peleiadeo Akhileos, 16
Mixed metaphors muddle middling minds, 106

Mortals may not match my magic, 72
Mothers mellow miracle mustard, 72, 107
Mr. Knox keeps his socks, 107
Mrs. Chip is very old, and when she settles
    down to stitch, 71
My song is of war and a man: a refugee by
    fate, 46
My soul is awakened, my spirit is soaring, 87

Nāsad āsīn no sad āsīt tadānī, 12
No one is an island entire of itself, 118
Not born to the forest are we, 55
Not like the brazen giant of Greek fame, 131
Numberless are the world's wonders, 84

O Captain! my Captain! 128
O Maker of the material world, thou Holy one!
    13
O noble Rome, 45
O radiant Apollo, 17
O Roma Nobilis! 45
Ode: Intimations of Immortality, 84
Oh Horace! Isn't it horrible when you're hot, 107
Oh, the sadness of her sadness when she's sad,
    105, 153
Old age is a flight of small cheeping birds, 144
On mules we find two legs behind, 72
Once I heard a mother utter, 68
Once upon a barren moor, 36, 101
One black beetle bled black blood, 67
One hen, two ducks, 148
One smart fellow, he felt smart, 74
Our birth is but a sleep and a forgetting, 84
Out of his hole to steal he stole, 36, 103
Out of the night that covers me, 129

Palatable prescriptions properly prescribed, 107
Pat's pa Pete poked a pea patch, 41
Peggy Babcock, 72
Penelope Cholmondely raised her azure eyes, 147
Peter has five prize pigs, 107
Pick a partner and practice passing, 154
Plain bun, plum bun, bun without plum, 70
Please bring the black-backed blank bank book
    back, 153

Please Paul, pause for applause, 72, 107
Please sell me some short silk socks, 74, 107
Pop bottles bottles in pop bottle shops, 35
Pure food for poor mules, 41
Put the cut pumpkin in a pipkin, 41, 72

Quick – Quack – Quock, 72

Real weird rear wheels, 154
Red leather, yellow leather, 71
Richard gave Robin a rap in the ribs, 72
Rick's spitz Fritz threw snits and fits, 74

Sarah sitting in her Chevrolet, 152
Season of mists and mellow fruitfulness, 88
Seven sleazy shysters in sharkskin suits, 152
Seventy shuddering sailors standing silent, 74
Several exceptionally technical secretaries, 107
Shadows on the wall, 57, 141
Shall I compare thee to a summer's day? 117
Shave a cedar shingle thin, 41
She let little Nellie run a little, 107
She saw the shiny soapy suds, 41, 107
She sells seashells on the seashore, 73
She stood on the balcony, 108
She stops at the shops where I shop, 108
Sheep shouldn't sleep in a shack, 41, 73, 108
Sheila Shorter sought a suitor, 103
Sheila uttered a sharp shrill shriek, 108
Sheila's Shetland pony shied, 73,
Shelly served chilly chili to silly Sally, 41
Shirley Simms shrewdly shuns sunshine,154
Shut up the shutters and sit in the shop! 73, 108
Sing, Goddess, Achilles' rage, 16
Sing, O daughter of heaven, 16
Six sick hicks nick six slick bricks, 73, 108
Snow and ice and silvered hedges, 41
Some seventy-six sad seasick seamen, 74, 108
Something there is that doesn't love a wall, 131
Something whistled past his head, 108
Sooty Sukey shook some soot, 74
Stanley sat sadly solitary, 73
Strode then the slaughter wolves, 49
Suddenly swerving, seven small swans, 73
Summer is coming, summer is coming, 25

Susan shineth shoes and socks, 73
Swart smirched smiths, smattered with smoke, 51
Swarte smekyd smethes, smateryd wyth smoke, 51
Swiftly slide the slippery snakes, 36, 73
Swim, Sam, swim! 38

Ted threw Fred three free throws, 74
Ten tiny toddling tots, 75, 108
The aged judge urges the jolly jury, 105
The Assyrian came down like the wolf on the fold, 95
The bleak breeze blights the bright broom blossom, 38, 40, 69, 154
The bold toad told the cold mole, 72
The city sweep shook his sooty sheet, 41
The drain in the train dripped again, 106
The fishermen say, when your catch is done, 22
The Lord is my Shepherd; I shall not want, 114
The miller shifts six sacks with care, 74
The morns are meeker than they were, 21
The old school scold sold the school coal scuttle, 73, 153
The outlook wasn't brilliant for the Mudville nine that day, 63
The quality of mercy is not strain'd, 116
The rain ceaseth and suffices us, 41
The school scold sold the school coal scuttle, 41
The seething sea ceaseth seething, 74, 107
The squire squealed with breathalyzing indignation, 108
The suitability of a suet pudding, 108
The sun was shining on the sea, 60
The unusual confusion surrounding the revision, 109
The wind was a torrent of darkness, 96
Then even nothingness was not, nor existence, 12
Theophilus Thistledown, 37, 75
There lived a sage in days of yore, 30
There lives in me an image, 11, 44, 78, 112
There was a Boy whose name was Jim, 59
There was a merchant in Bagdad, 92
There was a merry passenger, 149
There was a minimum of cinnamon, 152

There's a little metal kettle, 102
There's a slit in the sheet; the sheet is slit, 74
There's no need to light a night light, 102
These are these and those are those, 41
They have left the thrift shop, 154
Thin-skinned Slim, 74
This above all: to thine own self be true, 116
This is a story about four people, 154
This is the catastrophic hypothesis, 108, 154
This is the forest primeval, 20
This is the man for whom Africa, 46
This royal throne of kings, this scepter'd isle, 115
This we know: the earth does not belong to man, 125
Though I speak with the tongues of men and of angels, 114
Three blue beads in a blue bladder rattle, 70
Three fiddling pigs sat in a pit and fiddled, 40
Three free thugs set three thugs free, 74
Till Tom taught tact to Tim, 74, 108
Tim, the thin twin tinsmith, 41
Tim's black ticktock clock ticks, 41
Tim's twin sisters sing tongue twisters, 74
To every thing there is a season, 115
To look up at the sky, and behold, 83
To sit in solemn silence in a dull, dark dock, 153
To wonder at beauty, 11, 44, 79, 113
To you all honor O Olympia, 17
Tom bought some fine prime pink popcorn, 75
Tomorrow, and tomorrow, and tomorrow, 116
Top chopstick shops stock top chopsticks, 71, 108, 154
'Twas brillig, and the slithy toves, 29
'Twas the night before Christmas, 121
Twixt six thick thumbs stick six thick sticks, 153
Two roads diverged in a yellow wood, 85

Unless I am convicted by Scripture, 83
Up on their brooms the Witches stream, 54

Visible, invisible, a fluctuating charm, 26
Vivid, virtuous, vast and void, 109

We the People of the United States, 119
We'll begin with box, and the plural is boxes, 27

Whan that Aprill with his shoures soote, 50
What do we plant when we plant the tree? 24
When day comes we ask ourselves, 144
When in the Course of human events, 118
When we let freedom ring, 139
When you are standing at your hero's grave, 134
When, in disgrace with fortune and men's eyes, 117
Where ignorance predominates, 109
Whether the weather be fine, 33, 103
White cats, black cats, slick cats, slack cats, 40
Who is this who cometh as in conquest? 17
Whose woods these are I think I know, 56
Why do you cry, Willy? 75
Why is the worst verse worse than the first verse? 109
Why, man, he doth bestride the narrow world, 47
Wiles and snares and snares and wiles, 75, 109
Will you, William? 75
Willie found some dynamite, 37
Willie poisoned Auntie's tea, 37
Willie with a thirst for gore, 37
Willie's really weary, 75
Willie's whistle wouldn't whistle, 37
Wōdon þā wælwulfas (for wætere ne murnon), 49

You may write me down in history, 140
You've heard me, scornful, harsh, and discontented, 135
Your imbecilic mimicking is sickening, 72, 107

Made in the USA
Middletown, DE
06 June 2025

76584271R10093